©2010 DemiDec Corporation
1002 Wall Street
Los Angeles, CA 90015

Printed in the United States of America

2010
10 9 8 7 6 5 4 3 2 1

ISBN-13: 978-1-936206-13-1

DemiDec Cram Kits may be purchased at special high-quantity discounts for use in promotions or educational purposes. Please email us for more information at contact@demidec.com, or write to DemiDec at 1002 Wall Street, Los Angeles, CA 90015.

Editorial
Dean Schaffer, Editor
Daniel Berdichevsky, Editor-in-Chief

WHAT IS A CRAM KIT?
A Word from the Editor

BETTER THAN THE TEXTBOOK YOU NEVER READ

GETTING STARTED

Everyone says that if you want to do well on an exam, cramming is not the way to do it. But not everyone has used a Cram Kit.

If you're reading this, you've already taken a big step toward improving your score. Cram Kits are DemiDec's signature study guide, focused on two types of information:

1. That which is most likely to be tested.
2. That which is most likely to be forgotten.

This Cram Kit is *not* a textbook. It does not aim to teach you everything you could ever want to know about a subject. Rather, Cram Kits give you a focused, approachable, and engaging path to success on the AP exam—especially if you're crunched for time.

So what are you waiting for? Get cramming!

THE CRAM FAMILY – THE FIRST GENERATION

The first generation of the Cram Family delivers Cram Kits and Cram Cards in the following subjects:

AP Psychology	AP Calculus	AP Chemistry
AP Biology	SAT I	AP U.S. History
AP English Language	AP Economics (Micro and Macro)	AP Spanish Language

CRAMMING FOR SUCCESS
A Word from the Author

INTRODUCING THE CRAM KIT

WELCOME!

Welcome to the AP English Language Cram Kit! This guide will help you polish your ability to communicate and to analyze communication—and maybe have some fun along the way. In what other class do you get to analyze political cartoons, read stories, and criticize other people's ideas, all for course credit? Let's do it!

CRAM KIT ORGANIZATION: FOUR SECTIONS

1. Grammar

- Terms and definitions relating to grammar.
- You'll encounter a few direct questions asking you to identify parts of speech, sentence parts, and the like: the bulk of your grammar studying, however, should focus on learning to write grammatically.

2. Rhetorical Analysis

- Terms, definitions, and strategies for analyzing rhetoric.
- Again, you'll probably encounter direct questions that require your knowledge of these terms (many of the questions about the short passages will ask you to analyze how an argument is presented). More importantly, however, you'll want to internalize the meaning of these terms for use in your own essays— not as words, but as concepts. You may never be asked to define a fallacy, but you'll certainly want to avoid committing one.

ORGANIZATION, CONTINUED

3. Voice, Tone, and Style

- Terms and definitions relating to voice, tone, and style.
- You'll be asked to identify these in questions and reflect your knowledge of these in essays.

4. Literary Analysis

- Terms, definitions, and strategies for analyzing literary works.
- You may encounter multiple choice questions that require you to know these terms, or you may find it helpful to utilize these terms in your essays.

THE EXAM: THE BASICS

WHERE DOES MY SCORE COME FROM?

The AP English Language exam includes two parts: the multiple choice section and the essay section.

Multiple Choice 45%

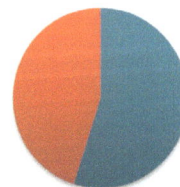

Free-Response 55%

CRAMMING FOR SUCCESS
How to Use This Book

A TERRIFIC TOOL

CRAMMING FOR SUCCESS

At their best, study aids clarify troublesome concepts or processes. (Can you squint at a dangling modifier, or dangle a squinting modifier?) At their worst, they confuse.

This book strives to outline the AP English Language curriculum in a clear and engaging manner. You've already gotten a taste of the format. Information is organized by

- Bullets, numbers, and checks
- Graphics (with pretty colors, of course)
- Tables and charts
- Bolded terms and headings

At the top of each page, you will find two headings. The larger heading, in all capital letters, refers to an overarching section or theme of the curriculum—think of it as a chapter of the book (on this page, "CRAMMING FOR SUCCESS"). The smaller heading refers to the specific topic of that page (on this page, "How to Use This Book"). These two headings will help you organize material thematically in your brain.

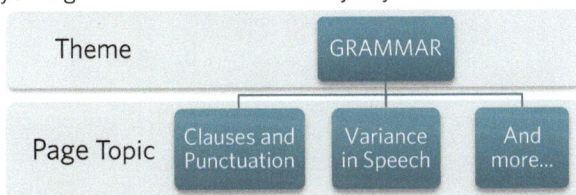

A quiz follows every page. It may cover material presented on the page previous or related information that wasn't included.

You'll find that the pages correspond to the percentages already mentioned—about a third of the pages, for example, deal with grammar.

CRUNCHING FOR SUCCESS

At the end of this book, you'll find a super-summary of the AP English Language course called the Crunch Kit. Use it as a quick reference, a last-minute refresher, or a high-speed review.

Following the Crunch Kit is the List of Lists, organized by topic. These lists introduce terms and their definitions that will probably be covered on the AP English Language exam. This section gives you a good chance to test your knowledge. Wait until you've reviewed the rest of the book and then see how many terms in the lists you can define without help. Most of the terms found in the lists are essential, so it's important to understand them fully before the test.

CRAMMING THE RIGHT WAY

KNOWING WHAT'S IMPORTANT

This book will help you with the major topics in the AP English Language course by reviewing terminology and other important points.

It's important to keep in mind that the concepts underlying the terminology are also important. There are many different kinds of fallacies, for example, and you might not be able to remember the names of all of them. But knowing how to avoid faulty reasoning will make your essays much stronger.

One could say the same thing for almost every topic in AP English Language. That doesn't mean you should ignore the details, though; just know where they come from.

THE MAJOR THEMES

Keep these concepts in mind while you're studying.

- **Rhetoric** is the art of persuasive communication
- A **fallacy** is a piece of shoddy reasoning; you'll want to identify these in other people's writing and avoid them in your own
- **Clarity** is the most important element of successful writing
- **Analysis** is unpacking *how* a writer makes a point, advances an argument, or tells a story
- Correct **grammar** is an integral part of clear writing
- **Voice** is the unique way in which a narrator speaks or writes
- **Tone** is the attitude an author has toward his or her topic

READY, GET SET, STUDY!

English is a fun subject to study because it's not all about right answers. (Okay, sometimes it is—there's only one correct definition of an independent clause.) But the bulk of your success on the English Language exam will stem from your ability to think critically, engage with text energetically, and communicate your ideas persuasively. Studying for English isn't usually about rote memorization; instead, it's about using the terms and concepts presented here as a foundation for your own thinking and writing. This is what makes English superior to all other subjects, regardless of the average salary of recently graduated English majors. Good luck, and happy studying!

GRAMMAR
Nuts and Bolts

PARTS OF SPEECH

EIGHT IS ENOUGH

Everything we say and write is composed of eight parts of speech.

THE PARTS OF SPEECH

Part of Speech	Function	Examples
1. Noun	Names a person, place, thing, or idea	Book, symphony, spider
2. Adjective	Modifies a noun	Gorgeous, humid, tedious
3. Verb	Expresses an action or a state of being	Walk, speak, study
4. Adverb	Modifies a verb, adjective, or adverb	Terribly, wonderfully, quickly
5. Conjunction	Links words, phrases, and clauses	And, or, thus
6. Pronoun	Replaces a noun	She, he, it
7. Preposition	Indicates the spatial, logical, or temporal relationship between a word and the rest of a sentence	On, under, through
8. Interjection	Doesn't fall into any of the other categories; often expresses emotion or surprise	Hey, whoa, gosh darnit!

SENTENCED!

The part of the sentence that modifies the subject is known as the **predicate**.

PARTS OF A SENTENCE

WHAT IS A SENTENCE?

A sentence contains a subject and a verb and expresses a complete thought.

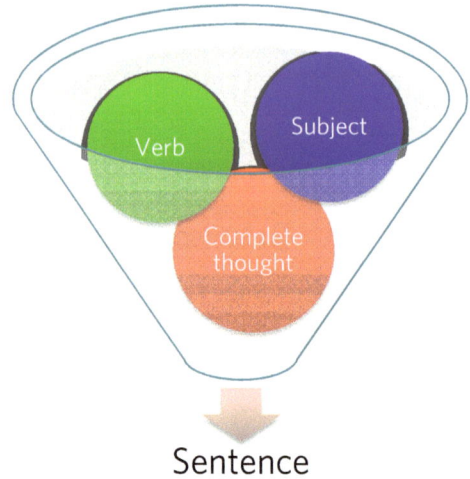

Sentence

TYPES OF SENTENCES

THREE OF A KIND

Sentences are categorized based on the number of independent and dependent clauses they contain.

Remember that independent clauses can stand on their own as complete sentences, whereas the needier dependent clauses cannot.

Simple Sentence	Complex Sentence	Compound Sentence
• Contains one independent clause • "I went to the store."	• Contains an independent clause • Joined by one or more dependent clauses • "When my pet guinea pig needed food, I went to the store."	• Contains two or more independent clauses • "My pet guinea peg did my homework for me, and I went to the store"

CRAM QUIZ
Nuts and Bolts

QUESTION 1

An adverb
(A) modifies a noun
(B) modifies a verb
(C) expresses action or states of being
(D) names a person, place, thing or idea
(E) expresses a spatial or temporal relation

QUESTION 2

The part of the sentence that modifies the subject is known as the
(A) verb
(B) noun
(C) adjectival clause
(D) predicate
(E) modifier

QUESTION 3

A sentence containing one independent clause and one or more dependent clause is called a(n)
(A) interrogative sentence
(B) declarative sentence
(C) simple sentence
(D) complex sentence
(E) compound sentence

QUESTION 4

Which of the following is an example of a preposition?
(A) tomorrow
(B) under
(C) corner
(D) afternoon
(E) all of the above

QUESTION 5

A dependent clause
(A) always begins with an adjective
(B) could stand alone as a complete sentence
(C) could not stand alone as a complete sentence
(D) always contains an independent clause
(E) always begins with an adverbial clause

QUESTION 6

By definition, a compound sentence:
(A) contains two or more independent clauses
(B) contains only two dependent clauses
(C) contains only one independent clause
(D) contains two subjects
(E) contains only one dependent clause

QUESTION 7

Which of the following is an example of an interjection?
(A) Stop!
(B) Gross!
(C) Whoa!
(D) Wait!
(E) Really?

QUESTION 8

How many parts of speech are there?
(A) four
(B) five
(C) six
(D) seven
(E) eight

ANSWERS

1. B
2. D
3. D
4. B
5. C
6. A
7. C
8. E

GRAMMAR
The Power of Verbs (And Adjectives)

ADJECTIVES

AWESOME ADJECTIVES

So, we know that adjectives modify nouns and give us more information about what the modified noun is like. Adjectives themselves are single words ("green," "ridiculous"), but often a string of words can function like an adjective.

Adjective Phrase

- A phrase that modifies a noun
- For example, "One *of Hilda's pet monkeys* bit me in the face"
- "Of Hilda's pet monkeys" modifies the noun "one"

Adjective Clause

- A clause that contains a subject and verb and modifies a noun:
- For example, "I'm studying for the AP, which is one reason *why I am stressed out*"
- "Why I am stressed out" modifies the noun "reason"

DON'T WORRY!

The important thing to remember is that an adjective modifies a noun—whether in clause form, phrase form, or as a single word.

But...

WHEN IS AN ADJECTIVE NOT AN ADJECTIVE?

When it's a noun. An adjective that functions as a noun is called an **adjectival noun.** Examples include "the rich," "the poor," "the young," and "the restless."

VERBS

VUNDERBAR VERBS

As we know, verbs express actions or states of being. English includes lots of different types of verbs, though. Here are a few.

- The **gerund**: any verb ending in the form –ing; in the previous phrase, "ending" is an example.
- The **auxiliary verb**: a verb that serves a linking function in a sentence; "to do," "to have," and "to be" are the auxiliary verbs in English
- The **participle**: a verb that functions as an adjective; for example, "I think the *sobbing* teacher is unhappy" ("sobbing" acts as an adjective which modifies "teacher")

TWO VERBS WITH ONE STONE

TRANSITIVE *VS. INTR*ANSITIVE

One important grammatical distinction is between transitive and intransitive verbs.

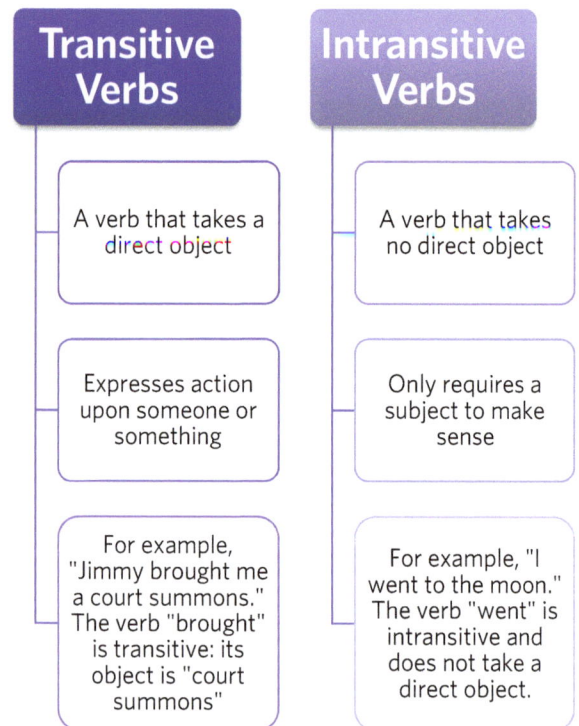

Transitive Verbs	Intransitive Verbs
A verb that takes a direct object	A verb that takes no direct object
Expresses action upon someone or something	Only requires a subject to make sense
For example, "Jimmy brought me a court summons." The verb "brought" is transitive: its object is "court summons"	For example, "I went to the moon." The verb "went" is intransitive and does not take a direct object.

CRAM QUIZ
The Power of Verbs (and Adjectives)

QUESTION 1

A verb that takes a direct object is called a(n)

(A) gerund
(B) participle
(C) transitive verb
(D) intransitive verb
(E) auxiliary verb

QUESTION 2

Which sentence contains an auxiliary verb?

(A) Jill sharpened her pencil.
(B) I am tired of studying.
(C) Larry kicked the ball.
(D) The laughing student aced the test.
(E) The Cram Kit gave me a paper cut.

QUESTION 3

An adjective clause contains

(A) a subject and modifies a noun
(B) a subject and a verb and modifies a noun
(C) a verb and modifies a noun
(D) neither a verb nor an adjective and modifies a noun
(E) a subject and a verb and starts with an adjective

QUESTION 4

An intransitive verb is a

(A) verb that modifies a noun
(B) verb that ends in "-ing"
(C) verb that takes no direct object
(D) linking verb
(E) verb that takes a direct object

QUESTION 5

A participle is a(n)

(A) verb ending in "-ing"
(B) verb that acts as an adjective
(C) clause that modifies a noun
(D) phrase that modifies a noun
(E) adjective that acts as a noun

QUESTION 6

Which of the following is an example of an adjectival noun?

(A) hideous
(B) green
(C) the table
(D) the bold
(E) A and B

QUESTION 7

A phrase that modifies a noun is called a(n)

(A) participial phrase
(B) adjective clause
(C) auxiliary verb
(D) adjective phrase
(E) gerund

QUESTION 8

In the sentence "I was up all night fighting zombies, which is one reason why I am tired," "why I am tired" is an example of a(n)

(A) adjective clause
(B) adjective phrase
(C) participle
(D) gerund
(E) auxiliary verb

ANSWERS

1. C
2. B
3. B
4. C
5. E
6. D
7. D
8. A

GRAMMAR
Words: From Antecedent to Zeugma

MOODS AND NOUNS

CRANKY VERBS

Like us, verbs have moods—and theirs are even trickier to decipher than ours are. These include:

Declarative	• Normal form of a verb • "I *walk* to school."
Conditional	• Expresses how things might happen or might have happened • "I *might walk* to school if it's not too cold."
Imperative	• Used when giving instructions • "*Drive* me to school."
Subjunctive	• Expresses a desire, wish, or command • "I know you want to walk to school. *Be that as it may*, it is too cold."
Indicative	• Expresses how things actually are • "I'm not *walking* to school."

The bottom line?
A verb's mood tells us whether something actually happened, might have happened, or should have happened.

ZOUNDS! SO MANY NOUNS!

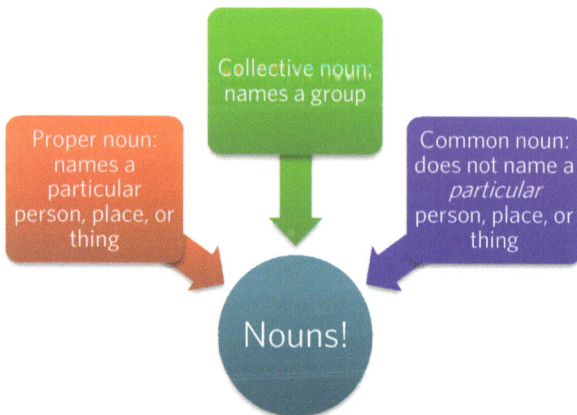

- **Collective noun:** names a group
- **Proper noun:** names a particular person, place, or thing
- **Common noun:** does not name a *particular* person, place, or thing

→ Nouns!

BUT DON'T FORGET!

✓ *Abstract nouns* refer to things that can't be perceived through the senses (for example, "meritocracy" and "justice")

✓ *Concrete nouns* refer to things that can be perceived through the senses (for example, words such as "apple" and "Wii")

TANTALYZING TERMS

I OBJECT!

Now that we've looked at transitive verbs, let's look at direct and indirect objects:

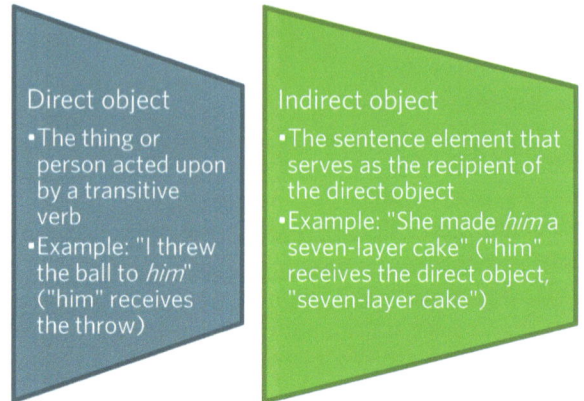

Direct object
- The thing or person acted upon by a transitive verb
- Example: "I threw the ball to *him*" ("him" receives the throw)

Indirect object
- The sentence element that serves as the recipient of the direct object
- Example: "She made *him* a seven-layer cake" ("him" receives the direct object, "seven-layer cake")

TRICKY TERMS TO REMEMBER

- **Affix:** something added to a root word (including suffixes, which are added to the end of a root word, and prefixes, which are added to the beginning of a root word; for example, the prefix "un" can combine with the root "truth" to make the word "untruth"

- **Antecedent:** the noun to which a pronoun refers; for example, in the sentence "Brunhilda has a pet dragon; she is so lucky!" "Brunhilda" is the antecedent to which the word pronoun "she" refers

- **Dangling modifier:** a writing error in which it is ambiguous what part of the sentence a word, phrase, or clause is modifying; for example, "having spent all night fending off zombies, coffee was needed": it sounds like coffee fended off zombies!

- **Infinitive:** the uninflected form of a verb; for example, "to give," "to hula-hoop"

- **Split infinitive:** when a word intervenes between "to" and the infinitive form of a verb; for example, "she wants to *quickly* sell her pet dragon"

- **Squinting modifier:** a modifier that is positioned in such a way that it may be taken to modify two words; for example, "Sally told me in geometry class Brunhilda naps": does Brunhilda nap in geometry class or does Sally talk in geometry class?

- **Quantifier:** an adjective that expresses numerical scope; for example, "I fended off *many* zombies"

- **Zeugma:** the use of a word to link two different phrases or words; for example, "he arrived in a limousine *and* a state of confusion"

CRAM QUIZ
Words: From Antecedent to Zeugma

QUESTION 1

Which of the following is an example of an abstract noun?

(A) ziglet
(B) unicorn
(C) table
(D) oligarchy
(E) cat

QUESTION 2

In the word "sub-conscious," "sub" is an example of which of the following?

(A) direct object
(B) affix
(C) zeugma
(D) quantifier
(E) infinitive

QUESTION 3

"Having wondered about his temperament, the dragon proved irritable." The preceding sentence includes an example of which of the following?

(A) dangling modifier
(B) the imperative mood
(C) split infinitive
(D) squinting modifier
(E) the conditional mood

QUESTION 4

"The zombies chased me through the village." In the preceding sentence, the word "me" functions as the

(A) zeugma
(B) direct object
(C) indirect object
(D) abstract noun
(E) affix

QUESTION 5

"Fred" is an example of a(n)

(A) proper noun
(B) concrete noun
(C) common noun
(D) abstract noun
(E) A and B

QUESTION 6

An adjective that expresses numerical scope is called a(n)

(A) zeugma
(B) dangling modifier
(C) affix
(D) squinting modifier
(E) quantifier

QUESTION 7

What is a split infinitive?

(A) the uninflected form of a verb
(B) a grammatical mistake in which another word intrudes between the word "to" and the infinitive form of the verb
(C) a grammatical mistake in which a modifier seems to modify two words
(D) a grammatical mistake in which it is ambiguous to what part of the sentence the modifier refers
(E) an infinitive after zombies get to it

QUESTION 8

In which of the following sentences does the word "me" function as the indirect object?

(A) "Sally and me talk a lot in math class."
(B) "The dragon swatted me with his paw."
(C) "Brunhilda brought me a bundt cake after the whole zombie thing."
(D) "The teacher told Sally and me to quiet down."
(E) None of the above

ANSWERS

1. D
2. B
3. A
4. B
5. E
6. E
7. B
8. C

GRAMMAR
Variance in Speech

CAN YOU REPEAT THE QUESTION?

YOU TALKIN' TO ME? ARE YOU TALKIN' TO ME?

Questions come in several forms—some aren't even followed by question marks, and some aren't seeking answers. Get it?

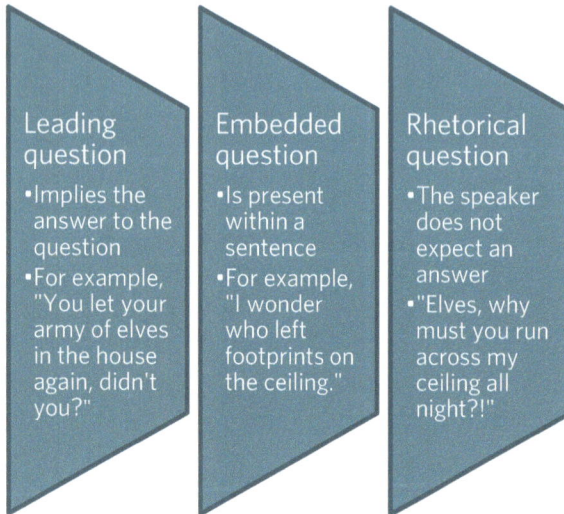

Leading question
- Implies the answer to the question
- For example, "You let your army of elves in the house again, didn't you?"

Embedded question
- Is present within a sentence
- For example, "I wonder who left footprints on the ceiling."

Rhetorical question
- The speaker does not expect an answer
- "Elves, why must you run across my ceiling all night?!"

THE FORCE OF DISCOURSE

There are two ways for a speaker or writer to report what he has heard or read: **direct discourse** and **indirect discourse.**

Direct discourse puts the statement that is being reported in quotations; for example, "I heard him say, 'Quiet down, elves, I think she can hear you.'"

Indirect discourse paraphrases the statement without the use of quotes; for example, "I heard him tell the elves to quiet down."

A MANNER OF SPEAKING

OH HEY, Y'ALL

You've probably noticed that people from different parts of the country speak differently but are mutually intelligible—and that individuals everywhere have particular patterns of speech. These variations are called **dialect** and **idiolect**.

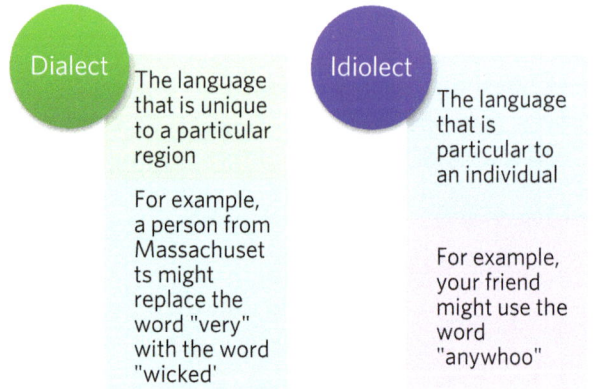

Dialect
The language that is unique to a particular region

For example, a person from Massachusetts might replace the word "very" with the word "wicked'

Idiolect
The language that is particular to an individual

For example, your friend might use the word "anywhoo"

VARIED VOICES

There are two different grammatical voices: **active voice** and **passive voice**.

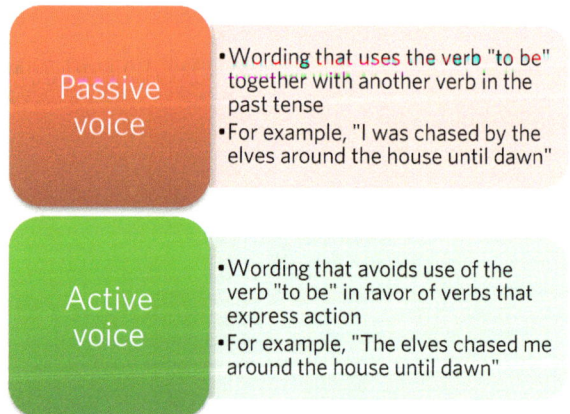

Passive voice
- Wording that uses the verb "to be" together with another verb in the past tense
- For example, "I was chased by the elves around the house until dawn"

Active voice
- Wording that avoids use of the verb "to be" in favor of verbs that express action
- For example, "The elves chased me around the house until dawn"

In formal writing, the active voice is most appropriate—it contributes to clarity and is a mark of strong writing. The passive voice, on the other hand, is generally a weaker way of wording things.

CRAM QUIZ
Variance in Speech

QUESTION 1

An individual's unique way of speaking is called a(n)

(A) active voice
(B) passive voice
(C) idiolect
(D) dialect
(E) rhetorical question

QUESTION 2

Dialect is

(A) an individual's unique way of speaking
(B) the way of speaking that is unique to a particular region
(C) a question that is implied in a sentence
(D) a question that does not seek an answer
(E) a question that suggests the answer

QUESTION 3

Construction that avoids use of the verb "to be" is called

(A) active voice
(B) idiolect
(C) embedded question
(D) passive voice
(E) leading question

QUESTION 4

Passive voice is

(A) a construction that avoids use of the verb "to be"
(B) a construction that uses the verb "to be"
(C) an individual's unique way of speaking
(D) the way of speaking that is unique to a particular region
(E) a question that is implied in a sentence

QUESTION 5

"I have to wonder why the elf footprints have not yet been cleaned up." The preceding is an example of a(n)

(A) rhetorical question
(B) leading question
(C) embedded question
(D) active voice
(E) passive voice

QUESTION 6

A question that suggests its own answer is called a(n)

(A) embedded question
(B) rhetorical question
(C) idiolect
(D) leading question
(E) dialect

QUESTION 7

A rhetorical question is a

(A) question implied within a sentence
(B) construction that uses the verb "to be"
(C) question that suggests its own answer
(D) construction that avoids use of the verb "to be"
(E) question that does not seek an answer

QUESTION 8

Reporting another statement without using quotations marks is called

(A) passive voice
(B) active voice
(C) direct discourse
(D) indirect discourse
(E) none of the above

ANSWERS

1. C
2. B
3. A
4. B
5. C
6. D
7. E
8. D

GRAMMAR
The Wacky and Wondrous World of Words!

ARTICLES

I DON'T GET THE REFERENCE

An article is a word that works with a noun to express the kind of reference the author is making, and may also express the volume of the reference.

Articles come in two varieties: **indefinite** and **definite**.

> I saw a yeti.

An indefinite article refers to any member of a group. In the sentence above, the indefinite article "a" implies that there are several yetis I could encounter.

> I saw the yeti.

A definite article refers to a particular member or members of a group. In this sentence, the definite article "the" implies that there is only one yeti I could encounter.

LET'S RECAP

Indefinite article	Definite article
Functions like an adjective	Functions like an adjective
Refers to any member(s) of a group	Refers to a particular member (or members) of a group

RELATIONSHIPS BETWEEN WORDS

SYNONYMS AND ANTONYMS

Antonym	Synonym
• A word that has the opposite meaning of another word	• A word that shares the same meaning as another word
• For example, "right" is an antonym of "wrong"	• For example, "bellicose" is a synonym for "pugilistic"

GOOD, BETTER, BEST

Words that are used to express the relationships between nouns are called **comparatives**.

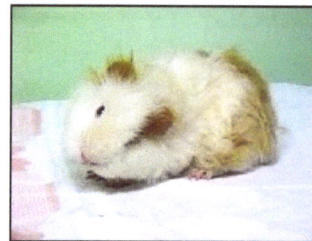

For example, in the sentence "My guinea pig is cuter than your child," the comparative "cuter" establishes the contrast between the cuteness of one thing (my guinea pig) and another thing (your child).

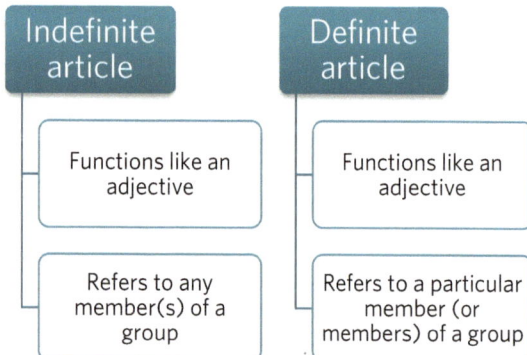

A **superlative** is an adjective that expresses the idea that something expresses a quality to the highest degree possible.

For example, in the sentence "My guinea pig is the cutest in the whole world," the superlative "cutest" establishes that my guinea pig has the quality of cuteness to the highest degree possible.

DemiDec

CRAM QUIZ
The Wacky and Wondrous World of Words!

QUESTION 1

Which of the followings pairs are antonyms of each other?

(A) red and yellow
(B) smart and silly
(C) guinea pig and elephant
(D) dissonance and consonance
(E) furious and outraged

QUESTION 2

A word that expresses a noun's possession of the highest degree of a given quality is called a(n)

(A) comparative
(B) indefinite article
(C) definite article
(D) superlative
(E) antonym

QUESTION 3

A word that is similar to another is called a(n)

(A) definite article
(B) superlative
(C) indefinite article
(D) antonym
(E) synonym

QUESTION 4

Both definite and indefinite articles

(A) refer to any member(s) of a group
(B) refer to particular member(s) of a group
(C) express gender
(D) function as nouns
(E) function as adjectives

QUESTION 5

A word that functions as an adjective and refers to any member or members of a group is called a(n)

(A) comparative
(B) indefinite article
(C) definite article
(D) superlative
(E) antonym

QUESTION 6

Which of the following sentences contains a definite article?

(A) I would love a peanut butter and baloney sandwich!
(B) These penguins are poorly dressed.
(C) Peanut butter and baloney sandwiches are delicious!
(D) I find the penguins' antics tedious.
(E) B and D

QUESTION 7

An article may express

(A) gender
(B) tense
(C) volume
(D) mood
(E) aspect

QUESTION 8

Which of the following words is a comparative?

(A) funnier
(B) bad
(C) good
(D) worst
(E) despicable

ANSWERS

1. D
2. D
3. E
4. E
5. B
6. B
7. C
8. A

GRAMMAR
Diction, Apposition, and Quotations

WORD ORIGINS & MODAL WRITING

DUELING DICTION

English is unique in that it borrows heavily from two languages: Latin and German. Interestingly, different kinds of words come from each of the two languages, giving English two dictions—**Latinate** and **Germanic**.

Latinate diction
- Words stemming from Latin
- Includes technical, medical, and scientific terms
- For example,"canine"

Germanic diction
- Words stemming from German
- Tend to be blunter and shorter than their Latin counterparts
- For example, "dog"

A LA MODAL

Modal writing is writing that tells what usually happened.
For example, "We'd spend every day trying to catch sight of the elves who, we suspected, were living in the ceiling."

WICKED AWESOME!

A **shibboleth** is a mannerism, usually linguistic, that reveals background. (Do you order a soda or a pop with your hoagie, sub, grinder, or hero?)

A WHOLE NEW WORD

Neologisms, or new words, can stem from a variety of sources:

- Pre-existing words (like "television," which comes from the word "vision" and the affix "tele-")

- Acronyms (like "laser," which stands for light amplification by stimulated emission of transmission)

- Other languages (like "bagel," which comes from the Yiddish *beygl*)

QUOTATIONS AND APPOSITION

TOO MUCH INFORMATION?

Apposition is the placement of two phrases together so as to give further information.

For example, the phrase "my brother, the liger trainer" gives us extra information about the speaker's brother.

QUOTE QUACKERY

You might think that quotes only involve...well, the words being quoted. But that's not quite accurate. Occasionally you'll encounter interpolation and broken quotations.

Interpolation is adding to a quote for clarity.

> He told me that he *"can neither confirm nor deny [the presence of elves]."*

In this sentence, "[the presence of elves]" is added in place of some word which would be ambiguous out of context (here, a word like "it").

A **broken quotation** is a quotation that is interrupted, usually by a dialogue tag.

> *"I wonder," he said, "whether chasing zombies is good cardiovascular exercise."*

In this sentence, "he said" interrupts the flow of the quotation to indicate the speaker.

CRAM QUIZ
Diction, Apposition, and Quotation

QUESTION 1

An appositional phrase

- (A) is an independent clause
- (B) clarifies a quotation
- (C) is composed of new words
- (D) gives additional information
- (E) always stems from Latinate diction

QUESTION 2

A broken quotation is a(n)

- (A) quotation that includes clarifying information
- (B) a quotation that contains an appositional phrase
- (C) a quotation that is interrupted by a dialogue tag
- (D) a quotation that employs Germanic diction
- (E) a quotation that has been ravaged by zombies

QUESTION 3

A neologism can emerge

- (A) from a combination of words
- (B) from another language
- (C) from an acronym
- (D) A and B
- (E) A, B, and C

QUESTION 4

Modal writing expresses

- (A) what will happen in the future
- (B) what usually happens or happened
- (C) what happened one time
- (D) what might happen
- (E) what might have happened

QUESTION 5

Latinate diction tends to include

- (A) words about geography
- (B) words about science
- (C) words about feelings
- (D) words about art
- (E) words about zombies

QUESTION 6

Words belonging to Germanic diction tend to be

- (A) long and elegant
- (B) short and frank
- (C) complicated and obscure
- (D) technical or scientific
- (E) in German

QUESTION 7

Which of the following sentences contains a shibboleth?

- (A) That sandwich was delicious, y'all.
- (B) Those zombies were ugly.
- (C) Don't point that laser at the zombie—it will anger him.
- (D) The zombie caught pneumonia.
- (E) My brother, the zombie, ate a sandwich.

QUESTION 8

Adding to a quote to clarify its meaning is called

- (A) explication
- (B) explanation
- (C) interpolation
- (D) inference
- (E) intrusive

ANSWERS

1. D
2. C
3. E
4. B
5. B
6. B
7. A
8. C

GRAMMAR
Clauses and Punctuation

PUNCTUATION NATION

MECHANICS

Mechanics are the technical details of writing.

Mechanics include grammar, punctuation, spelling, and even indentation. In fact, your essay scorers will be checking to see whether, among other things, you have a good grasp of the mechanics of standard English.

COMMA DRAMA

A **comma** (,)is a punctuation mark used to separate clauses, enclose parenthetical phrases or clauses, and separate coordinate adjectives.

An **Oxford comma** is a comma that is used before the conjunction in a list of three or more items.(Also called the **Harvard comma**; be careful not to confuse it with the Princeton diphthong or the Yale metrical foot.)

For example, "He bought eggs, milk**,** and bread." The Oxford comma comes after "milk" and before "and."

WHERE I'M COLON FROM

Colons and **semicolons** are punctuation marks that indicate that more information is to follow. For example:

- Colon: "Andrew is thrilled: today, he learned how to use a colon."
- Semicolon: "Students often anguish over semicolons; it is easy to see why."

SO WHEN DO I USE THEM?

Colon
A punctuation mark that indicates that more will follow

Usually followed by enumeration, expansion, or explanation

Semi-colon
A punctuation mark that is used to separate items in a list...

Or to separate two independent clauses

CLAUSING TROUBLE?

INDEPENDENT VS. DEPENDENT CLAUSES

An **independent clause** is one that can stand alone as a complete sentence.

Independent clause
A clause that can stand alone as a complete sentence

Dependent clause
A clause that cannot stand alone as a complete sentence

A **dependent clause** is one that cannot stand alone as a complete sentence; either it is missing a subject or a verb, or it does not express a complete thought.

CONTRACTION ACTION

A **contraction** is a word that is shortened by the elimination of internal letters.

For example, "it's" and "can't" are contractions.

CORRECT ME IF I'M WRONG

Hypercorrection is a grammatical mistake that stems, ironically, from an over-concern for grammatical correctness.

For example, people who are conditioned to avoid the word "me" might say that "Sally threw the ball to Robert and I"—even though "me" is correct!

BE CAREFUL...

...to avoid hyper-correction on the AP exam; remember to ask yourself whether the word you are writing is the sentence's direct object or indirect object.

FOR WHOM THE BELL TOLLS

Whom is a word that is subject to rampant hypercorrection. So when is it appropriate to use "whom"? "Whom" can be the object of a verb or preposition, or a relative pronoun. When you're confused, try substituting the word with "him/her" or "she/he." If "him/her" works, go with whom; if "she/he" is right, stick with who.

CRAM QUIZ
Clauses and Punctuation

QUESTION 1

A colon serves

(A) to separate items in a list
(B) to separate the final item in a list and a conjunction
(C) to indicate a pause before enumeration or explanation
(D) as a word that is shortened by eliminating internal letters
(E) as a clause that cannot stand alone as a sentence

QUESTION 2

A word that is shortened by eliminating internal letters is called a(n)

(A) contraction
(B) dependent clause
(C) independent clause
(D) hypercorrection
(E) semicolon

QUESTION 3

"*I went to the lemur store*, where the lemurs were escaping." In the preceding sentence, the italicized words are a(n)

(A) contraction
(B) hypercorrection
(C) dependent clause
(D) independent clause
(E) semicolon

QUESTION 4

A comma that immediately precedes a conjunction in a list is called a(n)

(A) Cambridge comma
(B) Oxford comma
(C) Harvard comma
(D) semi-comma
(E) B and C

QUESTION 5

A grammatical mistake arising from a heightened concern for grammatical correctness is called

(A) an independent clause
(B) hypercorrection
(C) Oxford comma
(D) semicolon
(E) colon

QUESTION 6

"I went to the store, *where I am hoping to buy a lemur.*" In the preceding sentence, the italicized words are a(n)

(A) contraction
(B) dependent clause
(C) independent clause
(D) Oxford comma
(E) hypercorrection

QUESTION 7

Which of the following sentences includes an example of hypercorrection?

(A) "Robert and I went to the store to buy a lemur."
(B) "Robert and me went to the store to buy a lemur."
(C) "Robert and Alan bought the lemur for Jeff and me, even though we did not ask for one."
(D) "Robert and Alan bought the lemur for Jeff and I, even though we are terrified of apes."
(E) "Robert and me are no longer fond of lemurs, after some unfortunate events at the store."

QUESTION 8

A semicolon is followed by a(n)

(A) dependent clause
(B) contraction
(C) hypercorrection
(D) Oxford comma
(E) a complete sentence

ANSWERS

1. C
2. A
3. D
4. E
5. B
6. B
7. D
8. E

GRAMMAR
Adverbs, Sentences, and Altering Quotations

MORE GRAMMAR DEFINITIONS

THE SEVEN ELLIP-SEAS

An ellipsis (…)is punctuation that indicates that words are missing (as from a quote).

For example, Anthony said, "I double-dog dare you to climb into the ferret house…It will be fun!" The ellipses indicate that some of the quotation—probably more reasons to climb into the ferret house—is missing.

DON'T BE SO NEGATIVE!

A **negative sentence** denies that a statement is true. For example, "I did not realize that the ferrets would react so poorly to being disturbed."

SUBORDINATING CONJUNCTIONS

A **subordinating conjunction** is a conjunction that introduces a dependent clause; for example, "although," "unless," and "therefore" are all subordinating conjunctions.

TO INFINITIVE AND BEYOND!

The **subject of an infinitive** is exactly what it sounds like. Don't confuse it with the subject of the sentence. For example, in the sentence "We saw Anthony flee the ferret house," the subject of the sentence is "we," but the subject of the unconjugated verb "flee" is "Anthony."

IT'S UNDERSTOOD

The **understood subject of a sentence** is one that is implied but not directly stated.

For example, in the sentence "Be careful not to provoke the pugilistic ferrets," there is an implied subject—you. Implied subjects often occur in the imperative (command) case.

SENTENCED TO LIFE

Interrogative sentence
- Poses a question
- For example, "How many elves live in your house?"

Exclamatory sentence
- Emphatically expresses emotion
- For example, "My goodness, that mumu is unflattering!"

Imperative sentence
- Expresses a command
- For example, "Go catch all of the ferrets that escaped."

TERMINOLOGY TO REMEMBER

THAT'S SO SIC

You've probably seen the word sic, usually situated between brackets in a quote. For example, my friend claims she "has eleven elf [sic] in her house." The "[sic]" indicates that the author quoting the statement knows that the quotation includes an error in the quotation and has included it anyways.

ADVERBS

An **adverb clause** is a clause that modifies a verb. For example, "I broke into the ferret house *because Anthony dared me*." "Because Anthony dared me" modifies "broke into."

An **adverb phrase** is a phrase that modifies a clause. For example, "The man who lives *next door* is a paid assassin." The phrase "next door" modifies the clause "the man who lives."

WHERE ARE YOUR MANNERS?

Clauses of manner are adverbial clauses that are used to talk about someone's behavior or how something is done. They are usually introduced by words like "like" and "as."

For example, "That baby talks *like a gremlin*."

PARENTHETICAL EXPRESSIONS

Parenthetical expressions contain non-essential information and do not significantly alter the meaning of a sentence.

For example, "The ferrets, *as far as we know*, are loose in the neighborhood."

TAKE IT TO THE LIMIT…ONE MORE TIME

A **limiting adjective** indicates *which one*, *how many*, or *whose*.

For example, "*my* neighbor, *the paid assassin*," or "*fourteen* belligerent ferrets."

CRAM QUIZ
Adverbs, Sentences, and Altering Quotations

QUESTION 1

An adjective that tells which one, whose, or how many is called a(n)

(A) adverb clause
(B) adverb phrase
(C) subject of the infinitive
(D) limiting adjective
(E) understood subject of a sentence

QUESTION 2

A sentence that poses a question is called a(n)

(A) exclamatory sentence
(B) interrogative sentence
(C) understood subject of a sentence
(D) imperative sentence
(E) ellipses

QUESTION 3

The word "sic" indicates that

(A) a subordinating conjunction will follow
(B) a subject is implied
(C) words are missing from the text
(D) a clause will follow
(E) irregularities in the text are directly quoted

QUESTION 4

Parenthetical expressions

(A) contain non-essential information
(B) precede a subordinating conjunction
(C) tell how many, which one, or whose
(D) tell how something is done or how someone behaves
(E) function as the understood subject of a sentence

QUESTION 5

Which of the following sentences has an understood subject?

(A) "I would prefer not to hold your baby; he looks like a gremlin."
(B) "That ferret is the feistiest of the bunch."
(C) "Did you see the ferret run into the store?"
(D) "Anthony is going to be in big trouble."
(E) "Don't go near the big ferret; he is in a poor mood."

QUESTION 6

Punctuation that demonstrates words are missing is called a(n)

(A) limiting adjective
(B) understood subject of a sentence
(C) ellipses
(D) sic
(E) adverb clause

QUESTION 7

Clauses that tell how something is done or how someone behaves are called

(A) adverb clauses
(B) adverb phrases
(C) limiting adjectives
(D) clauses of manner
(E) exclamatory sentences

QUESTION 8

Exclamatory sentences

(A) pose queries
(B) express emotion
(C) contain an understood subject
(D) begin with a subordinating conjunction
(E) tell how something is done or how someone behaves

ANSWERS

1. D
2. B
3. E
4. A
5. E
6. C
7. D
8. B

GRAMMAR
Predicates and Changes in Language

VARIATIONS IN ENGLISH

THE EVOLUTION OF WORDS

English is like a species—it evolves, mutates, and eventually becomes something new. Here are some terms dealing with how language changes:

NEW SLANG

Slang is a kind of language made up of short-term coinages and figures of speech. Can you dig it?

THE ORIGINS OF WORDS

Etymology is the study of the origins of words. The word comes from the Greek for "the study of the true sense of words." That's the etymology of the word "etymology." Does that blow your mind?

THAT'S JUST SEMANTICS

A **semantic change** is a change in a word's meaning. For example, "to starve" once meant "to die."

DIFFERENT KINDS OF ENGLISH

Non-standard English is a diverse set of conventions that is discernibly different from standard English (what you learn in school).

Informal English is casual English that is used in daily life; phrases such as "It's me" (instead of "It's I") have entered our vernacular.

IMPORTANT DETAILS TO REMEMBER

An **intensive pronoun** is a word used to emphasize the subject of a sentence. For example, "I heard the elves giggling *myself*."

WHY SO TENSE?

Past perfect tense relates two actions that happened in the past: "I threw a kiwi fruit at Hector, even though he *had told* me about his terrible fruit phobia."

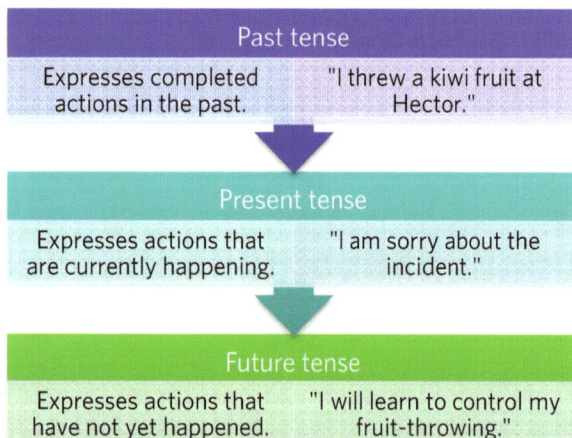

Past tense	
Expresses completed actions in the past.	"I threw a kiwi fruit at Hector."

Present tense	
Expresses actions that are currently happening.	"I am sorry about the incident."

Future tense	
Expresses actions that have not yet happened.	"I will learn to control my fruit-throwing."

PREDICATES AND PHRASES

PREDICATE

A **predicate adjective** follows a linking verb and tells us something about the subject. For example, "Hector is *covered* in kiwi fruit."

A **predicate nominative** follows a linking verb and tells us what the subject is. For example, "The kiwi fruit is *my favorite weapon*." ("Is" is the linking verb.)

GOING THROUGH A PHRASE?

An **intervening phrase** is a phrase following the subject. For example, "Hector, *covered in kiwi*, shook his fist at me."

TEST-TAKING TIP

Remember that the verb modifies the subject, no matter what the intervening phrase is doing. So don't get confused by a plural subject of an intervening phrase if the subject of your sentence is singular (or vice versa). For example, in the sentence "Melanie, accompanied by her two pet goats, looks silly," the verb "looks" should reflect the singular subject "Melanie."

PARALLEL UNIVERSE

Parallelism is when two or more sentence elements of equal importance are expressed similarly. For example, "I researched Malta—its *financial, cultural,* and *political institutions.*"

Lack of parallelism is a common grammatical mistake: "I researched Malta—its financial, cultural, and how its political institutions work."

CRAM QUIZ
Predicates and Changes in Language

QUESTION 1

Language composed of a diverse set of conventions that are discernibly different from standard English is called

(A) informal English
(B) non-standard English
(C) slang
(D) etymology
(E) parallelism

QUESTION 2

A phrase following a subject is called a(n)

(A) predicate nominative
(B) etymology
(C) parallelism
(D) future tense
(E) intervening phrase

QUESTION 3

A phrase that follows a linking verb and indicates what the subject is called

(A) past perfect tense
(B) predicate nominative
(C) predicate adjective
(D) an intensive pronoun
(E) parallelism

QUESTION 4

"I am bored" is an example of

(A) present tense
(B) past tense
(C) past perfect tense
(D) future tense
(E) none of the above

QUESTION 5

Parallelism is

(A) English used in daily life
(B) the study of word origins
(C) when two or more equal sentence elements are expressed similarly
(D) a phrase following a subject
(E) a phrase containing non-essential information

QUESTION 6

An intensive pronoun

(A) is a phrase containing non-essential information
(B) is a phrase following a subject
(C) follows a linking verb and tells something about the subject
(D) is a word that emphasizes the subject
(E) follows a linking verb and indicates what the subject is

QUESTION 7

A predicate adjective

(A) follows a linking verb and tells something about the subject
(B) follows a linking verb and indicates what the subject is
(C) emphasizes the subject
(D) contains non-essential information
(E) is a phrase following the subject

QUESTION 8

"I went to the movie because I had already gone to the zoo." "Had already gone" is an example of

(A) future tense
(B) past tense
(C) past perfect tense
(D) present tense
(E) none of the above

ANSWERS

1. B
2. E
3. B
4. A
5. C
6. D
7. A
8. C

RHETORICAL ANALYSIS
Introducing the Art of Argument

BASIC CONCEPTS

THAT'S ILLOGICAL, CAPTAIN KIRK!

Although you might think that the word "logic" refers to one kind of thinking, there are actually several types of logic you might encounter on the AP:

- **Associational logic** is an intuitive process of reasoning in which one idea, word, or concept leads to the next

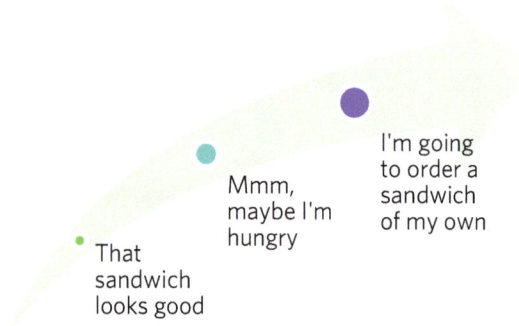

That sandwich looks good

Mmm, maybe I'm hungry

I'm going to order a sandwich of my own

- **Formal logic** is the rational process of reasoning and is also known as "ratiocination"

A = B + B = C ➡ A = C

For example,

That cat is black + Black cats are unlucky ➡ That cat is unlucky

SYLLOGISM

A **syllogism** is a form of argument in which a conclusion is inferred from two premises.

For example, "All men are mortal. Socrates is a man. Therefore, Socrates is a mortal." The first two sentences are premises, and the final sentence is a conclusion.

ARGUMENT STRUCTURES

DEDUCTIVE VS. INDUCTIVE REASONING

There are two primary modes of reasoning:

1. **Inductive reasoning** makes an observation and then draws a conclusion from it. You can think of inductive reasoning as "bottom-up" reasoning.

2. **Deductive reasoning** articulates a conclusion and then finds an example or examples to support it. You can think of deductive reasoning as "top-down" reasoning.

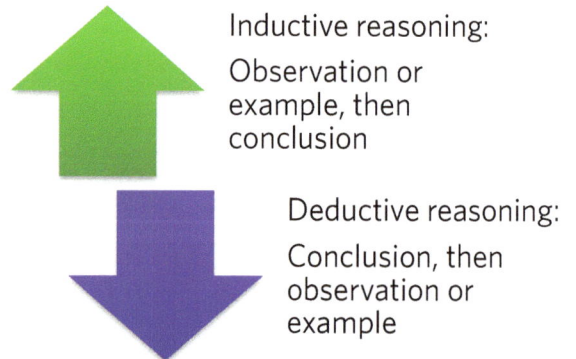

Inductive reasoning:
Observation or example, then conclusion

Deductive reasoning:
Conclusion, then observation or example

So, seeing a unicorn and then concluding that unicorns exist would be an example of inductive reasoning.

Concluding that a unicorn exists and then finding one to prove it would be an example of deductive reasoning.

Inductive-deductive reasoning moves from the particular to the general and back again, and **deductive-inductive reasoning**—you guessed it!—moves from the general to the particular and back again.

CRAM QUIZ
Introducing the Art of Argument

QUESTION 1

Which of the following is an example of associational logic?

(A) I found a coelacanth, and now I conclude that they still exist.
(B) A = B and B = C. Therefore, A = C
(C) This commercial reminds me that I need to buy Victoria's birthday present.
(D) I conclude that coelacanths still exist. I found one to prove it.
(E) None of the above

QUESTION 2

What is another word for "formal logic"?

(A) deductive reasoning
(B) inductive reasoning
(C) syllogism
(D) ratiocination
(E) associational logic

QUESTION 3

What is the structure of deductive reasoning?

(A) moving from the particular to the general
(B) moving from the general to the particular
(C) moving from the general to the particular and back again
(D) moving from the particular to the general and back again
(E) inferring a conclusion from two premises

QUESTION 4

"Taking my cactus out of the refrigerator seems to help it grow. I conclude that the refrigerator is not good for my cactus' growth." The preceding is an example of

(A) a syllogism
(B) inductive-deductive reasoning
(C) associational logic
(D) deductive reasoning
(E) inductive reasoning

QUESTION 5

Formal logic relies most on

(A) associations
(B) hunches
(C) rationality
(D) feelings
(E) zombies

QUESTION 6

Which of the following is an example of a syllogism?

(A) A = B and B = C. Therefore, A = C.
(B) A < B and B < C. Therefore, A < C.
(C) I'm hungry and want a sandwich; therefore, I will buy a sandwich.
(D) I saw a zombie; therefore, zombies exist.
(E) A and B

QUESTION 7

Inductive-deductive reasoning

(A) involves one concept or idea triggering another
(B) moves from the general to the particular and back again
(C) begins with a conclusion and leads to an observation or example
(D) begins with an observation or example and leads to a conclusion
(E) moves from the particular to the general and back again

QUESTION 8

A syllogism is an example of what kind of reasoning?

(A) inductive
(B) deductive
(C) ratiocination
(D) A and C
(E) none of the above

ANSWERS

1. C
2. D
3. B
4. E
5. C
6. E
7. E
8. D

RHETORICAL ANALYSIS
Tricks of the Trade

EMOTION, LOGIC, AND AUTHORITY

SOUND APPEALING?

In rhetoric, there are three primary methods that speakers and writers use to persuade their audience. These methods are **ethos** (appeal to authority), **logos** (appeal to logic), and **pathos** (appeal to emotion).

- Argument from **pathos**: You should buy Girl Scout cookies because Girl Scouts are adorable and they will be very, very sad if you do not buy their cookies. Do you want adorable children to be sad?
- Argument from **ethos**: As a former Girl Scout, I can tell you that Girl Scout cookies are the best cookies on the planet, so you should really buy some.
- Argument from **logos**: Girl Scout cookies are reasonably tasty and support a decent cause, so you should buy them.

CUE THE VIOLINS

Though **pathos** is an important rhetorical strategy, pathos can become **bathos** by going too far and becoming absurd.

For example, "You should buy Girl Scout cookies because Girl Scouts are adorable, and they put their sweat, tears, and piggy-bank savings into them."

TO READ IS TO BELIEVE

THE FUN OF PROPAGANDA LIVES AND CONQUERS!

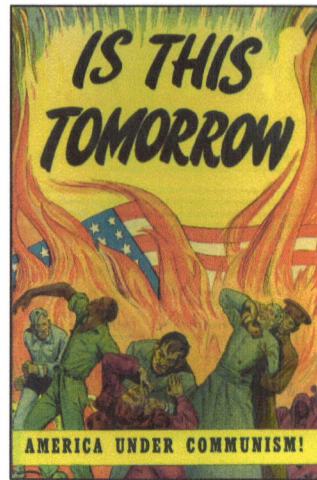

Propaganda is a didactic piece of work that seeks to persuade a reader to take a particular stance, often through the selective inclusion of information.

For example, giving only data that supports your conclusion—even if there is some data that does not—is a propaganda tool. So is this comic book from 1947.

CIRCLING THE WAGONS

Often, writers try to get their audiences to care about the kind of people who accept—or don't accept—the argument being advanced.

Bandwagon appeal relies on the notion that something should be done or believed because many people already do or believe it.

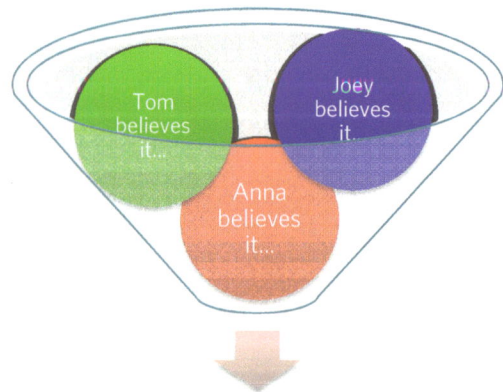

Bandwagon appeal!

The **ad hominem fallacy** is a rhetorical mistake in which the reader or speaker attacks his or her opponent personally, instead of the opponent's argument. For example, "Your views on universal healthcare are untenable because you are ugly."

CRAM QUIZ
Tricks of the Trade

QUESTION 1

When an appeal to emotion goes too far and becomes absurd, it is called

(A) bandwagon appeal
(B) ad hominem fallacy
(C) ethos
(D) pathos
(E) bathos

QUESTION 2

"You should vote for Candidate X because I've known him for 30 years and I can tell you that he is a terrific leader." The preceding is an example of

(A) ethos
(B) bathos
(C) logos
(D) pathos
(E) ad hominem fallacy

QUESTION 3

Arguing that a person should support your position because a lot of people already do is called

(A) logos
(B) ad hominem
(C) pathos
(D) bathos
(E) bandwagon appeal

QUESTION 4

Selectively including only information that supports your argument might be a form of

(A) logos
(B) pathos
(C) bathos
(D) propaganda
(E) ad hominem fallacy

QUESTION 5

What is an appeal to logic called?

(A) ethos
(B) bathos
(C) pathos
(D) ad hominem fallacy
(E) logos

QUESTION 6

Which of the following is an example of the ad hominem fallacy?

(A) "You shouldn't support my opponent's because there is no data to back up his claims."
(B) "You shouldn't support my opponent's position because his position will lead to children being sad."
(C) "You shouldn't support my opponent's position because he is a hypocritical windbag."
(D) "You shouldn't support my opponent's position because your favorite celebrity doesn't."
(E) None of the above

QUESTION 7

What is the primary goal of propaganda?

(A) to entertain
(B) to convince
(C) to provoke discussion
(D) to raise questions
(E) to encourage critical thinking

QUESTION 8

What is a fallacy?

(A) a rhetorical mistake
(B) an inaccurate conclusion
(C) a poor choice of words
(D) a bad spelling error
(E) a delusion

ANSWERS

1. E
2. A
3. E
4. D
5. E
6. C
7. B
8. A

RHETORICAL ANALYSIS
Examining Arguments

MORE RHETORICAL STRATEGIES

SNOBS AND MOBS

The broad rhetorical categories of **logos**, **ethos**, and **pathos** can encompass a variety of other rhetorical strategies and appeals.

For example,

Ethos	Pathos
Plain-folks appeal	Loaded words
Snob appeal	Glittering generalities

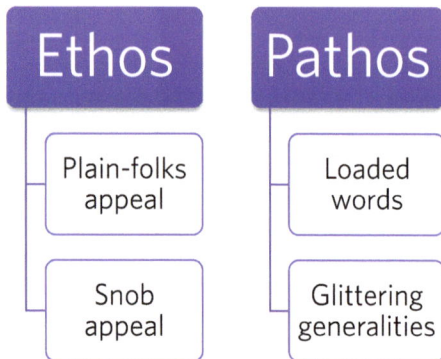

Using **plain-folks appeal** means implying that the "common man" uses a particular product or endorses a particular position, whereas **snob appeal** means implying that the elite use a particular product or endorse a particular position.

Both plain-folks appeal and snob appeal are examples of the rhetorical strategy of **ethos**, since both invoke the authority of the people supporting the argument.

An **appeal to authority** is an appeal to credible, external, established sources, which makes it a kind of ethos. (Think of celebrities admonishing you to buy particular brands of water.)

Personal myth is a self-concept that a writer creates and employs to enhance his or her image.

Loaded words are words with strong emotional associations—"choice" and "life," for example, are such words. **Glittering generalities** are loaded words that elicit strongly positive emotional connotations—such as "all-American."

When you encounter loaded words of any kind, you can guess that the rhetorical strategy of **pathos** is at work.

MORE RHETORICAL PROBLEMS

FIENDISH, FEARSOME FALLLACIES

In addition to the **ad hominem fallacy**, there are whole slew of other rhetorical mistakes you may encounter—or make!—on the AP Exam.

The **either-or fallacy**, for example, falsely assumes that there are only two potential solutions to a problem.

Either A Or B

The **cause-and-effect fallacy**—which is also known as conflating **correlation** and **causation**—occurs when the author assumes that one event caused another just because the two events occurred consecutively.

CORRELATION, ALL I EVER WANTED

For example, if you happened to stub your toe at the moment your computer crashed, and assumed that the computer crashed because it felt sorry for you (or was laughing at you).

Jargon is overly-technical, inaccessible language, and is best avoided (unless you're writing for a medical journal).

Archaic language is old-fashioned language. Verily, I do aver that any use of Such Language will be deemed Preposterous, Overblowne, and Most Fearfully Loathsome by any Youthe who might Encounter it.

Circular reasoning means giving no particular reason to support your claim:

This sandwich is delicious! → Because it's so delicious → I mean, delicious → Yum yum yum → Therefore, this sandwich is delicious →

CRAM QUIZ
Examining Arguments

QUESTION 1

What is a loaded word?

(A) a word with a strong emotional connotation
(B) an ambiguous word
(C) a word that is used incorrectly
(D) a word with a strongly negative emotional connotation
(E) a word that is too fancy for the context

QUESTION 2

Which is an example of circular reasoning?

(A) "I like sandwiches because everybody likes sandwiches."
(B) "I like sandwiches because my dear old granny liked sandwiches."
(C) "I like sandwiches because they are tasty and nutritious."
(D) "I like sandwiches because I like sandwiches."
(E) "I like sandwiches because all of my favorite athletes like sandwiches."

QUESTION 3

Words with strongly positive connotations are called

(A) bandwagon words
(B) ad hominem words
(C) loaded words
(D) generalities
(E) glittering generalities

QUESTION 4

Using glittering generalities is an example of which of the following?

(A) loaded words
(B) bandwagon appeal
(C) pathos
(D) ethos
(E) A and C

QUESTION 5

"Ordinary people with common sense, just like you, enjoy Cedric's Cereals." The preceding is an example of

(A) cause-and-effect fallacy
(B) bandwagon appeal
(C) plain-folks appeal
(D) circular reasoning
(E) snob appeal

QUESTION 6

What is another term for the cause-and-effect fallacy?

(A) either-or fallacy
(B) conflating correlation and causation
(C) circular reasoning
(D) bandwagon appeal
(E) ad hominem fallacy

QUESTION 7

Persuading an audience that the elite use a certain product or hold a certain belief relies on

(A) bandwagon appeal
(B) snob appeal
(C) plain-folks appeal
(D) ad hominem fallacy
(E) either-or fallacy

QUESTION 8

Plain-folks appeal is an example of what rhetorical strategy?

(A) bandwagon appeal
(B) pathos
(C) ethos
(D) logos
(E) bathos

ANSWERS
1. A
2. D
3. E
4. E
5. C
6. B
7. B
8. C

RHETORICAL ANALYSIS
Testable Terms

THE TRICKIEST OF THE BUNCH

BIG WORDS FOR SIMPLE IDEAS

In argumentation, everything has its own term—and a lot of these terms are very long words. Here's a quick review of some of the trickiest of the bunch:

Tapinosis
- Undignified language that demeans or person or thing

Hypocrisis
- Imitating an opponent's manner to mock him or her

Categoria
- Direct indictment of an opponent's faults

Auxesis
- Gradual heightening of words' intensity of meaning

Antirrhesis
- Rejecting an argument because of its triviality or moral wrongness

NOT TO MENTION...
- The beastly **bdelygmia:** a litany of insults
- The sinister **synathroesmus:** a listing of adjectives
- The terror of a **totalizing statement**: an assertion that deals in absolutes (often using words like "always" and "never")

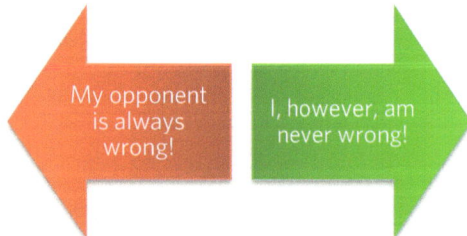

My opponent is always wrong!

I, however, am never wrong!

A BIT LESS TRICKY, BUT HUGELY IMPORTANT

CONCESSIONS AND MISREPRESENTATIONS AND DIGRESSIONS, OH MY!

Here's a quick review of some of the concepts you're most likely to encounter on Test Day.

- **Concession:** admitting a disputed point
- **Digression:** a passage that is not tightly tied to the overarching theme, plot, or argument of a work
- **Unity:** the coherence of a work
- **Thesis:** the argument that a piece of writing articulates or defends
- **Jeremiad:** a screed that seeks to denounce a person, place, thing, or idea
- **Context:** the background in which an event or fact is situated
- **Righteous indignation**: moralistic anger
- **Us vs. Them** argumentation: form of argument which denigrates the other side of the debate

Us: Delightful!

Them: Dreadful!

- **Misrepresentation of references**: taking your opponent's words out of context
- **Refutation:** when a speaker or writer anticipates and rebuts an opponent's position

CRAM QUIZ
Testable Terms

QUESTION 1

What is the term for a gradual heightening of the intensity of words' meaning?

(A) synthroesmus
(B) auxesis
(C) tapinosis
(D) bdelygmia
(E) antirrhesis

QUESTION 2

What is a concession?

(A) a litany of insults
(B) a list of adjectives
(C) a passage that doesn't relate to the rest of the piece
(D) an admission of a disputed point
(E) a rebuttal

QUESTION 3

What is the term for a direct indictment of an opponent's faults?

(A) refutation
(B) tapinosis
(C) categoria
(D) concession
(E) digression

QUESTION 4

"I hate sandwiches because they are always, always so terrible" is an example of what?

(A) tapinosis
(B) categoria
(C) Us vs. Them
(D) totalizing statement
(E) hypocrisis

QUESTION 5

Which of the following is a litany of insults?

(A) bdelygmia
(B) synthroesmus
(C) tapinosis
(D) auxesis
(E) antirrhesis

QUESTION 6

What is the term for taking one's opponent's points out of context?

(A) tapinosis
(B) Us vs. Them
(C) auxesis
(D) misrepresentation of references
(E) antirrhesis

QUESTION 7

Which of the following is the term for imitating an opponent's manner?

(A) antirrhesis
(B) tapinosis
(C) categoria
(D) bdelygmia
(E) hypocrisis

QUESTION 8

Using undignified language to demean someone or something is called

(A) hypocrisis
(B) categoria
(C) tapinosis
(D) antirrhesis
(E) auxesis

ANSWERS

1. B
2. D
3. C
4. D
5. A
6. D
7. E
8. A

RHETORICAL ANALYSIS
Augmenting Your Argument

RHETORICAL POSSIBILITIES

ABOUT THE AUTHOR

Often, authors bring themselves into their arguments; this technique can be an important part of establishing credibility. Here are a few ways they do it.

- An **anecdote** is a brief story, usually illustrative; for example, I might back up my theory about the coming mummy takeover by referencing a story about encountering one of them in the grocery store

- A **personal myth** is a self-concept that a writer or narrator presents; this can be an integral element of the rhetorical strategy of *ethos* because it establishes a relationship between the speaker or writer and the audience

I WILL DIE IF I HAVE TO LEARN ONE MORE AP TERM

Hyperbole is the rhetorical strategy of using exaggeration. For example, "Studying for the AP exam bores me to tears."

DON'T GET CONFUSED...

Don't mix up **explication** and **exposition.** Explication the process of making the implicit explicit. Exposition is a piece of writing that offers explanation.

TEST-TAKING TIP
On Test Day, you may be asked to "explicate" a text. This just means you're being asked to analyze the text—what is the writing doing, and how?

...AND PROBLEMS

RHETORICAL MISTAKES

Be careful to avoid the following pitfalls while formulating your AP essays:

1. A tautology is when an author states something twice unnecessarily. For example, "single bachelor" is a redundant term because the word "bachelor" necessarily contains the concept of "single." In logic, a tautology reflects circularity of argument; in rhetoric, it indicates a weakness of style.

2. Begging the question is assuming your conclusion in the course of your argument. ("My opponent is wrong because it is in his nature always to be wrong.")

3. Dogmatism is arrogance or stubbornness in asserting an opinion.

Artistic Appeal	Inartistic Appeal
•In rhetoric, a statement that makes a rational appeal	•In rhetoric, a statement of hard evidence
•Cannot be proved or disproved by facts	•Can be proved or disproved by facts
•For example, "we should enact universal healthcare"	•For example, "A majority of Americans support the elements of universal healthcare"

ARGUMENTS

SUBJECT TO DEBATE

There are several different kinds of arguments you might encounter on the AP Exam (or utilize in your own writing):

Causal argument
- Advancing an argument about the underlying cause of a certain phenomenon

Argument of evaluation
- Advancing a position about the merits of a certain policy, proposal, or position

Argument of definition
- Advancing a position about the way we understand or categorize something

CRAM QUIZ
Augmenting Your Argument

QUESTION 1

A statement that relies on hard evidence is called a(n)

(A) artistic appeal
(B) inartistic appeal
(C) dogmatism
(D) tautology
(E) causal argument

QUESTION 2

An argument of definition

(A) advances a proposition about what course of action should be taken
(B) advances a proposition about a policy
(C) advances a proposition about the underlying cause of a certain phenomena
(D) advances a proposition about how we should understand or categorize something
(E) advances a proposition about a plan

QUESTION 3

Personal myth is a(n)

(A) appeal to emotion
(B) appeal to logic
(C) appeal to hard evidence
(D) appeal to authority
(E) appeal to rationality

QUESTION 4

In rhetoric, an anecdote often serves what purpose?

(A) To entertain the audience
(B) To support an argument with statistics
(C) To illustrate a point
(D) To offer an inartistic appeal
(E) To annoy the readers

QUESTION 5

A tautology is

(A) stubbornness or arrogance in asserting an opinion
(B) assuming your conclusion in the course of your argument
(C) repeating information unnecessarily
(D) a statement that relies on hard evidence
(E) a statement that relies on rationality

QUESTION 6

An argument that advances a proposition about the underlying cause of a certain phenomenon is called a(n)

(A) inartistic appeal
(B) argument of definition
(C) causal argument
(D) argument of evaluation
(E) artistic appeal

QUESTION 7

Explication is

(A) making the implicit explicit
(B) exploring the underlying cause of a phenomena
(C) introductory information
(D) advancing a proposition about how something should be categorized or understood
(E) arguing from hard evidence

QUESTION 8

What is begging the question?

(A) raising a query
(B) unnecessarily repeating information
(C) pleading with a question to do you a favor
(D) assuming your conclusion in the course of making your argument
(E) reaching a conclusion from evidence

ANSWERS

1. B
2. D
3. D
4. C
5. C
6. C
7. A
8. D

VOICE, TONE, AND STYLE
The Basics

TONE AND STYLE

DON'T YOU GIVE ME THAT ATTITUDE

A writer's **attitude** is his or her opinion of—and feelings toward—the topic at hand.

In part, attitude is conveyed through **voice**—the distinctive thought and language patterns of a first-person narrator.

Voice, in turn, is tied closely to **point of view**, the emotional and situational position from which the speaker narrates the story or piece.

POINT OF VIEW
The point of view is the position from which the speaker or writer narrates.

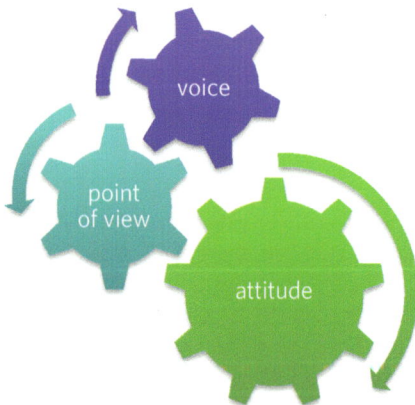

These elements combine to communicate the narrator's feelings about the described events or content.

SOME SYLISTIC STRATEGIES

1. **Meiosis** is under-emphasizing the importance of something for rhetorical effect (as in, "It's only a flesh wound!")
2. **Sarcasm** is saying or writing the opposite of what is meant, sometimes for comic effect; I'm sure this term will take you awhile to figure out
3. A **tongue-in-cheek** tone is one that is wry or mildly ironic. ("Thank you very much for your gift of an empty yogurt carton for my birthday; I only had 11 and needed to complete my set.")

VOICE

THERE IS DICTION IN THE SPACE BETWEEN

Authors make choices about what words to use to convey their points. The selection and arrangement of words in a piece is called **diction**.

Diction, for example, can be elevated, flowery, economical, or full of **colloquialisms**, commonly used figures of speech.

Word choice is an author's selection of words and is an element of diction.

In formal writing, it's important for diction to match subject matter. If it doesn't, the author may find him- or herself **overwriting**.

Overwriting
•The use of language that is unnecessarily wordy or elaborate

Economy
•Using only the necessary number of words to communicate a point

A **non sequitur** is a comment with no meaning relative to what preceded it. Best to avoid these altogether in your AP essays. Is it just me, or does that cloud look like a snowboarding weasel?

TEST-TAKING TIP
Overwriting your AP essays may help you fill up pages more quickly, but it won't impress the scorers. Stick to words that you are confident using, and your arguments and points will flow more naturally.

CRAM QUIZ
The Basics

QUESTION 1

Meiosis is
- (A) saying the opposite of what is meant
- (B) using the necessary number of words to make a point
- (C) under-emphasizing something for rhetorical effect
- (D) using elaborate language
- (E) a wry or biting tone

QUESTION 2

Saying the opposite of what is meant is called
- (A) sarcasm
- (B) meiosis
- (C) economy
- (D) overwriting
- (E) voice

QUESTION 3

On the AP Exam, you should
- (A) be economical whenever possible
- (B) overwrite whenever possible
- (C) use sarcasm whenever possible
- (D) employ a tongue-in-cheek tone whenever possible
- (E) B and C

QUESTION 4

Word selection and arrangement is called
- (A) voice
- (B) style
- (C) attitude
- (D) diction
- (E) tone

QUESTION 5

Using the necessary number of words to communicate a point is called
- (A) overwriting
- (B) sarcasm
- (C) meiosis
- (D) economy
- (E) tongue-in-cheek tone

QUESTION 6

How does an author communicate attitude?
- (A) through voice
- (B) through point of view
- (C) through spelling
- (D) through font
- (E) A and B

QUESTION 7

What is the term for a narrator's fictional—or rhetorical—vantage point?
- (A) tone
- (B) attitude
- (C) style
- (D) point of view
- (E) voice

QUESTION 8

A narrator's voice is
- (A) his or her level of understatement
- (B) his or her dialogue
- (C) his or her word selection and arrangement
- (D) his or her feelings about the subject
- (E) his or her unique patterns of thinking and speaking

ANSWERS

1. C
2. A
3. A
4. D
5. D
6. E
7. D
8. E

VOICE, TONE, AND STYLE
Tone, Point of Telling, and Phrasing

TONE AND POINT OF TELLING

WHAT IS YOUR OBJECTIVE?

There are two different ways of dealing with facts: **objectively** and **subjectively**.

Objective
- Neutral
- Dealing with facts without bringing to bear one's own experiences and biases

Subjective
- Particular to a specific individual
- Dealing with facts by bringing to bear one's own experience

UNDERSTATEMENT

Understatement is the rhetorical strategy of restraint, or treating something with less intensity than might be expected. Similar to meiosis, understatement can sometimes be used for comedic effect.

ONCE UPON A TIME, IN A LAND FAR, FAR AWAY...

Narrators have an almost endless variety of options for when to begin and how to tell their stories.

The **point of telling** is the chronological vantage point from which a narrator (whether in fiction or non-fiction) tells his or her story.

A **tone of retrospection** communicates that the point of telling is far removed from the events in the story ("Many years ago, when I was a lad...").

A tone that is somewhat less retrospective may communicate that the events are situated in the relatively recent past ("Last summer, something strange happened that I'm still trying to understand...")

A story or essay written in the present tense, of course, communicates that the point of telling and the events in the story are occurring simultaneously—in other words, the events are being narrated as they happen.

SUBTLETY AND PHRASING

SUBTLETY

A **subtlety** is a finely drawn distinction or nuance. In Ernest Hemingway's short story "Hills Like White Elephants," the subject of the couple's conversation—abortion—is dealt with so subtly that many students need to read the story twice to understand it.

Hemingway was a master of subtlety

DO YOU WANT TO REPHRASE YOUR STATEMENT?

Phrasing is the way sentences are worded. Be attentive to your phrasing on the AP essays; your top priority should be clarity.

STRINGY STYLE

"**Stringy style**" is the overuse of words like "and" and "so." You want to avoid this style on the AP, and instead write concise sentences, and avoid run-ons, and avoid needless verbosity, so you can do well!

TYPES OF TONE

DON'T TAKE THAT TONE WITH *ME*, MISSY

Tone is an author's attitude toward his or her subject matter.

- A **tone of nostalgia**, for example, is an attitude of longing for things past
- A **tone of horror**, on the other hand, is an attitude of revulsion or fear

Tone can be communicated by dwelling on words or images that evoke a certain set of emotions.

CRAM QUIZ
Tone, Point of Telling, and Phrasing

QUESTION 1

The overuse of words like "and" and "so" is called

(A) tone
(B) tone of nostalgia
(C) stringy style
(D) tone of horror
(E) understatement

QUESTION 2

Bringing to bear one's own personal experiences is called

(A) subjectivity
(B) objectivity
(C) tone of nostalgia
(D) word choice
(E) understatement

QUESTION 3

The chronological vantage point from which a story is told is called

(A) tone of retrospection
(B) point of telling
(C) subjectivity
(D) objectivity
(E) subtlety

QUESTION 4

The way sentences are arranged is called

(A) tone
(B) voice
(C) phrasing
(D) word choice
(E) point of telling

QUESTION 5

Understatement is

(A) the overuse of words like "and" and "so"
(B) the use of restraint for rhetorical effect
(C) a sense of longing for the past
(D) a sense of revulsion or fear
(E) the way sentences are arranged

QUESTION 6

Subtlety is

(A) bringing to bear one's own personal experiences
(B) the use of restraint for rhetorical effect
(C) a sense of longing for the past
(D) the way sentences are arranged
(E) a finely drawn distinction

QUESTION 7

Objectivity is

(A) a sense of revulsion or fear
(B) a sense of longing for the past
(C) reporting facts without referencing one's own personal experience
(D) reporting facts while referencing one's own personal experiences
(E) the way sentences are arranged

QUESTION 8

A point of telling situated far in advance of the events in the story has a

(A) tone of nostalgia
(B) tone of horror
(C) subtlety
(D) tone of retrospection
(E) phrasing

ANSWERS

1. C
2. A
3. B
4. C
5. B
6. A
7. C
8. D

LITERARY ANALYSIS
The Reach of Words

REFERENCES

ALLUSION

Authors can include references to figures, works, places, or events in order to draw a comparison or a contrast. These references are called **allusions**:

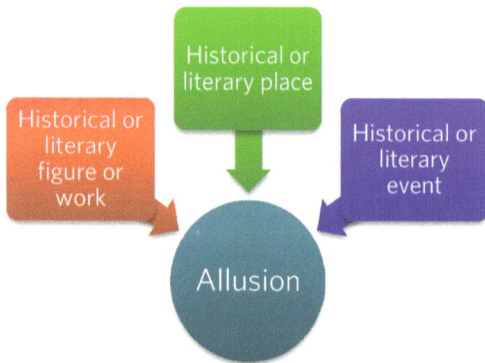

ALLEGORY AND CONCEIT

Sometimes, many elements in a work correspond to historical or literary places, figures, events, or works. This kind of work is called an **allegory**.

An allegory's **conceit**, or overarching premise, usually involves a relationship between the reality of the work and some outside reality—as in *The Lion, The Witch, and The Wardrobe*, in which the story's events parallel events in the Bible.

CONNOTATION NATION

A SHACK BY ANY OTHER NAME

You might think that words with the same meanings elicit the same reactions—but that's not quite right. A word's **denotation** is its literal meaning or definition. A word's **connotation** is the set of feelings or associations that a word evokes.

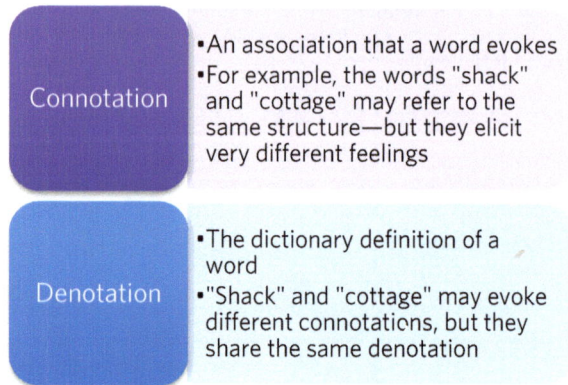

Connotations aren't the only way to play with words, however. A **double entendre** is a word used to apply to two meanings. Not to be confused with...

INNUENDO

Something that is implied, not explicitly stated. I wonder if any of this will be on the AP?

AND FINALLY...

GESTALT

The overall effect of a work.

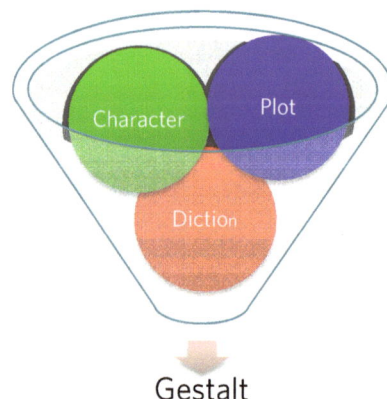

Gestalt

CRAM QUIZ
The Reach of Words

QUESTION 1

What is innuendo?

(A) the definition of a word
(B) a reference to a literary or historical figure, place, or event
(C) a word with two meanings
(D) the associations evoked by a word
(E) something that is implied but not directly stated

QUESTION 2

The words "house" and "home"

(A) have different double entendres
(B) have different allusions
(C) have different gestalts
(D) have different connotations
(E) have different denotations

QUESTION 3

A work in which events, figures, or places correspond to other events, figures, or places is called a(n)

(A) allusion
(B) allegory
(C) conceit
(D) connotation
(E) gestalt

QUESTION 4

When a word is used in order to play with dual meanings, it is called

(A) allusion
(B) double entendre
(C) allegory
(D) connotation
(E) gestalt

QUESTION 5

The overall effect of a work is called

(A) innuendo
(B) allusion
(C) gestalt
(D) connotation
(E) double entendre

QUESTION 6

A reference to a literary or historical figure, place, or event is called a(n)

(A) allusion
(B) connotation
(C) gestalt
(D) denotation
(E) double entendre

QUESTION 7

The overarching premise of a work is called a(n)

(A) allusion
(B) allegory
(C) conceit
(D) denotation
(E) gestalt

QUESTION 8

Which of the following best defines the term "denotation"?

(A) a reference to a literary or historical figure, place, or event
(B) the overarching premise of a work
(C) the overall effect of a work
(D) the definition of a word
(E) the associations evoked by a word

ANSWERS

1. E
2. D
3. B
4. B
5. C
6. A
7. C
8. D

LITERARY ANALYSIS
The Mechanics of Plot

RULES OF THE FRAME

THERE'S MORE THAN ONE WAY TO TELL A STORY...

Although most fiction adheres to certain conventions, there is a lot of variety in the ways that stories are told.

Some stories involve a **frame story**, a narrative structure which includes other, usually shorter, stories within a larger matrix. (In *The Canterbury Tales*, for example, an overarching frame story serves as the opportunity for the characters to tell their tales.)

Stories may also contain sub-plots, secondary stories that exist within the broader narrative arc.

TEST-TAKING TIP
Don't confuse the sub-plot with the story that exists within a frame story. The story that exists within the frame story is usually the central one—as is the story that exists around the sub-plot.

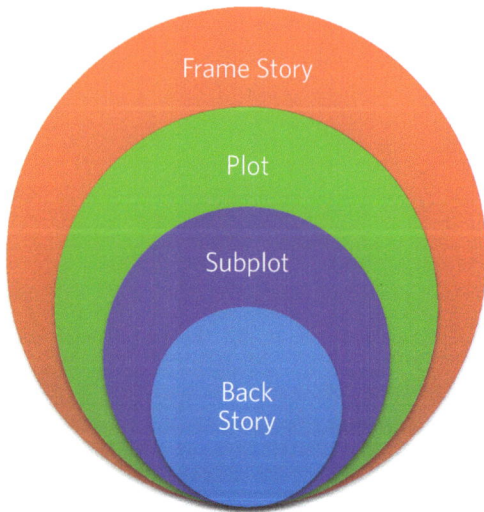

Frame Story

Plot

Subplot

Back Story

In media res is the literary strategy of starting a story in the middle of the action, rather than at the very beginning of everything. Homer's *Iliad* famously uses this technique.

TROPES, CONVENTIONS, AND CLICHES

BUT MANY STORIES ARE SUSPICIOUSLY SIMILAR

Over the course of human history, people have written *a lot* of stories. So it's not surprising that certain relationships, figures, and turns of phrase seem to come up again and again...and again...and again...

- A **cliché** is a turn of phrase that has become so common as to be hackneyed (think of such descriptions as "her skin was fair as snow")

- An **idiom** is a figure of speech that is not easily translated into another language (for example, "he put his best foot forward")

- A **trope** is a figure of speech or a figure of thought that arises over and over in literature (think of the hero-fool or the prostitute with the heart of gold)

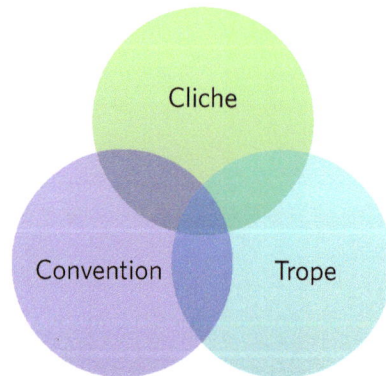

Cliche

Convention

Trope

- A **convention** is similar to a trope; this term refers to a familiar theme or rule of literature (the conventions of comedy, for example, dictate that a comedy must have a reasonably happy ending)

- A **stock situation** is a situation that is commonly found in literature (think of intrepid orphans making their way in the world)

CRAM QUIZ
The Mechanics of Plot

QUESTION 1

A familiar rule of literature is called a(n)

(A) trope
(B) cliché
(C) convention
(D) in media res
(E) frame story

QUESTION 2

In media res is

(A) a recurring theme in literature
(B) the story that surrounds other narratives
(C) a secondary plot within the primary plot
(D) when an author begins a story in the middle of the action
(E) a turn of phrase that is so common it has become hackneyed

QUESTION 3

A recurring figure of speech or figure of thought in literature is called a(n)

(A) subplot
(B) trope
(C) cliché
(D) convention
(E) frame story

QUESTION 4

A situation that recurs over and over in literature is called a(n)

(A) in media res
(B) cliché
(C) stock situation
(D) frame story
(E) subplot

QUESTION 5

The central narrative usually exists

(A) within the subplot, if there is one
(B) within the frame story, if there is one
(C) around the subplot, if there is one
(D) A and B
(E) B and C

QUESTION 6

"Her eyes were dark as night." The preceding line is an example of a(n)

(A) cliché
(B) frame story
(C) trope
(D) convention
(E) in media res

QUESTION 7

What is a subplot?

(A) the overarching story within which smaller narratives exist
(B) a plot that recurs over and over in literature
(C) a plot which starts in the middle of the action
(D) a plot that has been used so often it is hackneyed
(E) a secondary plot that exists within the primary plot

QUESTION 8

The mad scientist is an example of a(n)

(A) in media res
(B) stock situation
(C) trope
(D) subplot
(E) frame story

ANSWERS

1. C
2. D
3. B
4. C
5. B
6. A
7. E
8. C

LITERARY ANALYSIS
Symbol and Theme

SYMBOLS

MAPLE LEAVES AND SETTING SUNS

A **symbol** is an image, word, or phrase that contains meaning beyond its literal meaning.

There are two types of symbols—conventional symbols and universal symbols.

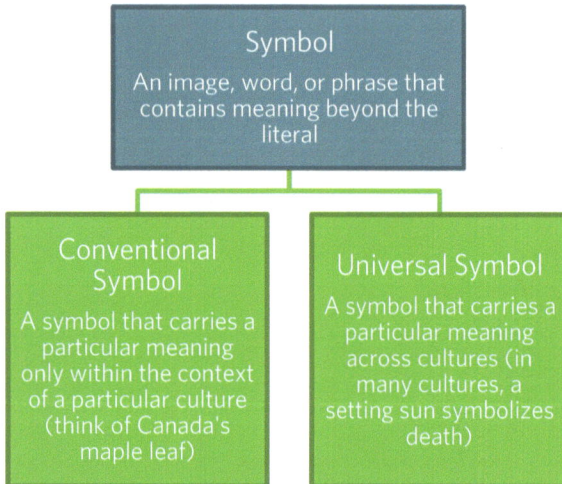

Symbol
An image, word, or phrase that contains meaning beyond the literal

Conventional Symbol
A symbol that carries a particular meaning only within the context of a particular culture (think of Canada's maple leaf)

Universal Symbol
A symbol that carries a particular meaning across cultures (in many cultures, a setting sun symbolizes death)

DON'T BE SO CRITICAL!

There are a variety of vantage points from which critics approach interpretations to literature.

- **Moral literary criticism** examines the moral implications of a text—does it impart morally sound messages?
- **Freudian literary criticism** approaches the text from a Freudian perspective, utilizing aspects of dream analysis
- **Formalist literary criticism** examines the inherent features of a text, such as grammar, syntax, tropes, narration, and character
- **Feminist literary criticism** examines the text from a feminist perspective: how does the author represent women, if at all?
- **Marxist literary criticism** examines the text from a class perspective: how does the author represent members of different social classes, if at all?
- **Deconstructionist literary criticism** seeks to examine the contradictions underpinning a work of literature

THEMES

I THEMED A THEME OF DAYS GONE BY

Character and plot exist to communicate a piece of literature's idea—that is, what the piece of literature is really all about.

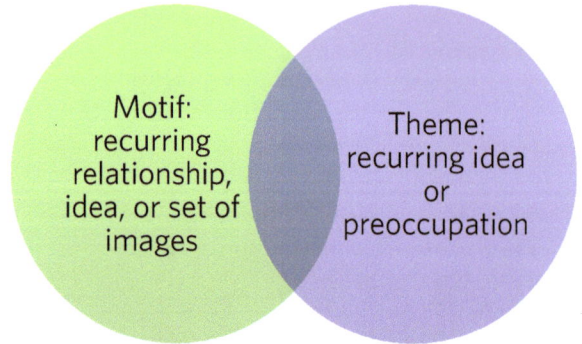

Motif: recurring relationship, idea, or set of images

Theme: recurring idea or preoccupation

Motifs are similar to themes, but a motif can refer to a set of relationships or images as well as ideas.

OTHER TERMS

NEGATIVE CAPABILITY

Keats coined this term to refer to receptivity to ambiguity or mystery. A writer, he said, "must be capable of being in uncertainties, mysteries, doubts, without any irritable reaching after fact and reason."

OBJECTIVE CORRELATIVE

T.S. Eliot coined this term to refer to the idea that the correct image can serve as a formula for emotion—better than words about emotions could.

SEMANTICS

The study of meaning—in everyday usage, this term often refers to a misunderstanding stemming from word connotation or selection.

INTERPRETATION

Plain and simple: a general explanation of a text's meaning.

CRAM QUIZ
Symbol and Theme

QUESTION 1

The examination of a text's meaning is called

(A) interpretation
(B) objective correlative
(C) negative capability
(D) theme
(E) motif

QUESTION 2

A conventional symbol

(A) generates emotion better than a description of emotion
(B) exists in ambiguity and mystery
(C) carries meaning across cultures
(D) carries meaning only in a particular culture or cultures
(E) is a recurring preoccupation within a text

QUESTION 3

A literary approach that examines the role and representation of women is called

(A) Freudian literary criticism
(B) Deconstructionist literary criticism
(C) feminist literary criticism
(D) moral literary criticism
(E) formalist literary criticism

QUESTION 4

A symbol that carries meaning across cultures is called a(n)

(A) motif
(B) universal symbol
(C) conventional symbol
(D) theme
(E) objective correlative

QUESTION 5

Criticism that approaches text from a class perspective is called

(A) feminist literary criticism
(B) Marxist literary criticism
(C) deconstructionist literary criticism
(D) formalist literary criticism
(E) moral literary criticism

QUESTION 6

Which of the following is a recurring preoccupation or idea within a text?

(A) theme
(B) motif
(C) objective correlative
(D) A and C
(E) A and B

QUESTION 7

Negative capability is

(A) the idea that an image can generate emotion better than descriptions of emotion
(B) the idea that text should be approached from a Freudian perspective
(C) the motif of a text
(D) the theme of a text
(E) the idea that a writer needs to exist in ambiguity and mystery

QUESTION 8

Deconstructionist literary criticism

(A) approaches the text from a feminist perspective
(B) examines the inherent features of the text
(C) seeks to examine the contradictions underpinning the text
(D) examines the moral implications of the text
(E) examines the class implications of the text

ANSWERS

1. A
2. D
3. C
4. B
5. B
6. E
7. E
8. C

LITERARY ANALYSIS
Mockery and Satire

THE MANY KINDS OF MOCKERY

IMITATION IS THE SINCEREST FORM OF MOCKERY

Writers have a variety of ways to mock, skewer, satirize, and have fun at the expense of other people, ideas, and literary works. Here's a quick review:

- To **lampoon** is to skewer or satirize
- A **satire** is a work that criticizes the failings of a person, society, or institution by way of ridicule

Criticizes failings + Ridicules = Satire

- A **parody** is a spoof: a text that mocks another by imitating many of its features
- A **pastiche** is a parody on a smaller scale
- A **travesty** is talking or writing about an elevated subject in crass or demeaning language

WHAT DO ALL OF THESE TECHNIQUES HAVE IN COMMON?

They often share a reliance on **irony**, the use of words to convey the opposite of what is literally meant.

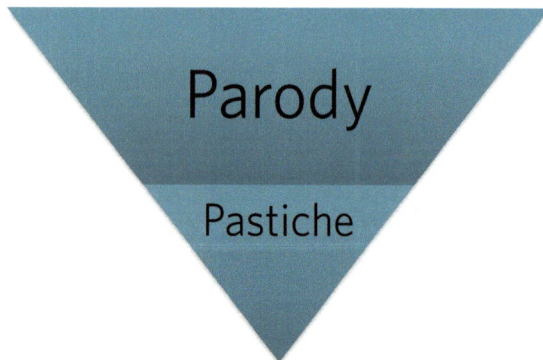

Parody

Pastiche

CASE STUDY: A MODEST PROPOSAL

LET THEM EAT...BABIES?

A MODEST PROPOSAL...

Written in 1729, Jonathan Swift's essay's full title is actually "A Modest Proposal: For Preventing the Children of Poor People in Ireland from Being a Burden to their Parents or Country, and for Making Them Beneficial to the Public." Aside from demonstrating the absurdity of ridiculously long titles, "A Modest Proposal" is extremely important because it is an early example of Western satire.

In the essay, Swift suggests that the poor people of Ireland sell their children to rich people—for food.

Swift supports his argument with many details, such as a list of suggestions for how children might be best be prepared and an accounting of the financial soundness of his suggestion.

As part of this satire, Swift takes aim at a host of targets:

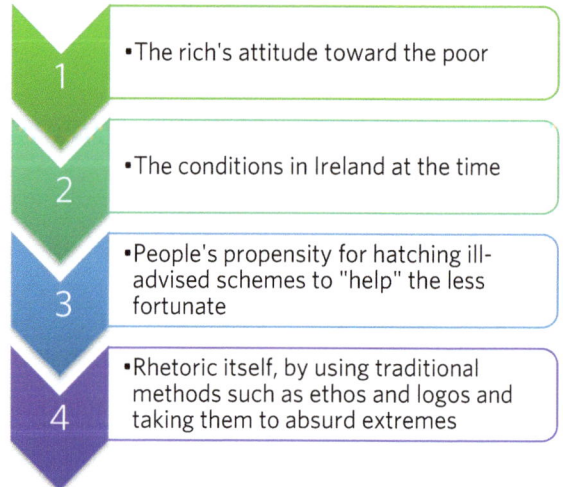

1. The rich's attitude toward the poor
2. The conditions in Ireland at the time
3. People's propensity for hatching ill-advised schemes to "help" the less fortunate
4. Rhetoric itself, by using traditional methods such as ethos and logos and taking them to absurd extremes

Finally, Swift denigrates the solutions he actually wishes to advance, like levying extra taxes and buying only domestically made products. (Funny how the arguments stay the same...)

CRAM QUIZ
Mockery and Satire

QUESTION 1

Jonathan Swift's "A Modest Proposal" is an early example of Western

(A) travesty
(B) parody
(C) satire
(D) lampoon
(E) pastiche

QUESTION 2

"A Modest Proposal" targets

(A) the rich's attitude toward the poor
(B) the poor
(C) schemes to "help" the poor
(D) the behavior of poor people
(E) A and C

QUESTION 3

What is parody?

(A) using demeaning words to discuss an elevated subject
(B) a spoof
(C) a piece that criticizes through ridicule
(D) a spoof on a small scale
(E) irony

QUESTION 4

In "A Modest Proposal," Swift's intention was probably

(A) to educate people about the unexamined potential of Irish children
(B) to offer a provocative solution to poverty
(C) to criticize poor people for being poor
(D) to criticize society on multiple levels
(E) to persuade society to adopt his stated proposal

QUESTION 5

A spoof that is small in scale is called a

(A) travesty
(B) pastiche
(C) parody
(D) satire
(E) lampoon

QUESTION 6

A satire

(A) ridicules to entertain
(B) ridicules to enlighten
(C) ridicules to criticize
(D) ridicules to elevate
(E) ridicules to be mean

QUESTION 7

Using demeaning words to discuss an elevated subject is called a

(A) travesty
(B) satire
(C) pastiche
(D) parody
(E) lampoon

QUESTION 8

To lampoon is to

(A) imitate
(B) use demeaning words about an elevated subject
(C) parody on a small scale
(D) spoof
(E) skewer or satirize

ANSWERS

1. C
2. E
3. B
4. D
5. B
6. C
7. A
8. E

LITERARY ANALYSIS
Case Study: *Hamlet*

THE BASICS

HISTORICAL CONTEXT

Written in Modern English, Shakespeare's *Hamlet* is part of the English language canon—in other words, if you've taken a class on British literature, or great literature in general, you've probably read (or been told to read) this play.

Hamlet is based on a number of fables. The title character himself resembles the "hero-fool" character, who is widespread among stories told in the Indo-European Language Group.

ELEMENTS OF CHARACTER

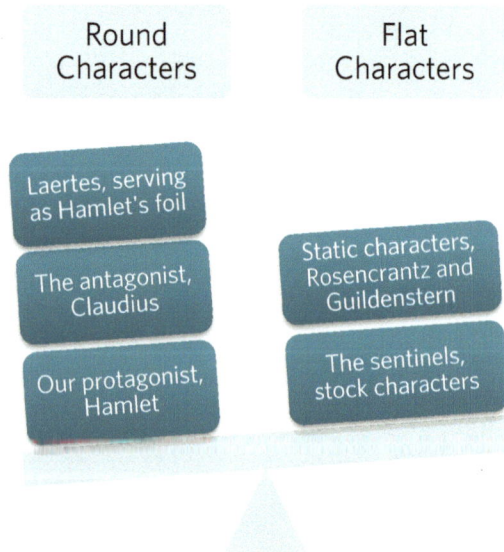

Round Characters	Flat Characters

Laertes, serving as Hamlet's foil

The antagonist, Claudius

Our protagonist, Hamlet

Static characters, Rosencrantz and Guildenstern

The sentinels, stock characters

IRONY

Hamlet includes three different kinds of irony.

1. *Verbal irony*: a character says the opposite of what he means—as when Hamlet says, "What a piece of work is man!"

2. *Situational irony*: a circumstance unfolds in an unexpected way, as when Hamlet declines to kill Claudius during prayer—and we later learn that Claudius wasn't praying at all.

3. *Dramatic irony*: the audience or readers know things that the characters do not—as when the audience is aware of Laertes's poison-tipped sword, but Hamlet is not.

PLOT VOCABULARY IN ACTION!

ELEMENTS OF PLOT

- The **catalytic event**—the sighting of Hamlet's father—instigates the action of the play
- **Rising action**—the events that precede the climax—includes the growing concern over Hamlet's madness and the death of Polonius
- Along the way, Hamlet directly addresses the audience in a famous **soliloquy**
- Meanwhile, a **subplot** involving a possible Norwegian invasion unfolds
- Political tensions between Denmark and Norway serve as the broader **enveloping action**
- The **climax** accompanies the fencing duel between Laertes and Hamlet
- The **epiphany** arrives when Claudius' plot is revealed
- Fortinbras' brief eulogy for Hamlet comprises the **falling action**
- **Stasis**, or harmony, is restored after the deaths of Hamlet, Gertrude, Claudius, and Laertes

ALL THE WORLD'S A STAGE

The scene in which Gertrude and Claudius watch and comment on the play-within-a-play is a moment of **meta-fiction**: a story about a story.

COMPONENTS OF TRAGEDY

MORE THAN A SAD STORY

Hamlet's tragic structure isn't just about the title character's moping. Remember that a tragedy is defined as a story in which a character's downfall arises from a tragic flaw (a flaw which might have led to greatness in other circumstances). In *Hamlet*, the title character's tendency to self-examine and self-question renders him unable to act.

Tragic Flaw ➕ Downfall 🟰 Tragedy

CRAM QUIZ
Case Study: *Hamlet*

QUESTION 1

The character who challenges the protagonist is called a(n)

(A) stock character
(B) antagonist
(C) foil
(D) static character
(E) jerk

QUESTION 2

Enveloping action is

(A) the events preceding the climax
(B) the events following the climax
(C) the event that sets the plot in motion
(D) the political and historical context in which the plot unfolds
(E) the events that conclude the plot

QUESTION 3

A stock character is a

(A) central character
(B) character who undergoes a change
(C) character who does not undergo a change
(D) fully developed character
(E) character type that frequently occurs in fiction

QUESTION 4

Fiction about fiction is called

(A) super-fiction
(B) meta-fiction
(C) uber-fiction
(D) sub-fiction
(E) epi-fiction

QUESTION 5

The catalytic event

(A) always involves a clash between the protagonist and antagonist
(B) immediately follows the climax
(C) concludes the story
(D) begins the story
(E) immediately precedes the climax

QUESTION 6

The audience knowing something that a character does not is known as

(A) dramatic irony
(B) situational irony
(C) Socratic irony
(D) verbal irony
(E) irony of fate

QUESTION 7

An epiphany is a(n)

(A) change
(B) reversal
(C) realization or revelation
(D) conflict
(E) instigation

QUESTION 8

In fiction, stasis is

(A) boredom
(B) equilibrium or harmony
(C) a conflict or challenge
(D) a speech delivered when a character is alone
(E) taking a part for a whole

ANSWERS

1. B
2. D
3. E
4. B
5. D
6. A
7. C
8. B

LITERARY ANALYSIS
Case Study: *Hamlet*'s "To Be or Not to Be" Speech

WHAT *IS* THE QUESTION, ANYWAYS?

THE FAMOUS SPEECH

To be, or not to be: that is the question:
Whether 'tis nobler in the mind to suffer
The slings and arrows of outrageous fortune,
Or to take arms against a sea of troubles,
And by opposing end them? To die: to sleep;
No more; and by a sleep to say we end
The heart-ache and the thousand natural shocks
That flesh is heir to, 'tis a consummation
Devoutly to be wish'd. To die, to sleep;
To sleep: perchance to dream: ay, there's the rub;
For in that sleep of death what dreams may come
When we have shuffled off this mortal coil,
Must give us pause: there's the respect
That makes calamity of so long life;
For who would bear the whips and scorns of time,
The oppressor's wrong, the proud man's
contumely,
The pangs of despised love, the law's delay,
The insolence of office and the spurns
That patient merit of the unworthy takes,
When he himself might his quietus make
With a bare bodkin? who would fardels bear,
To grunt and sweat under a weary life,
But that the dread of something after death,
The undiscover'd country from whose bourn
No traveller returns, puzzles the will
And makes us rather bear those ills we have
Than fly to others that we know not of?
Thus conscience does make cowards of us all;
And thus the native hue of resolution
Is sicklied o'er with the pale cast of thought,
And enterprises of great pitch and moment
With this regard their currents turn awry,
And lose the name of action.

I THINK WE'RE ALONE NOW?

Interestingly, though this speech is considered a **soliloquy**, *Hamlet is not actually alone onstage at the time of its delivery.*

A POETIC AND RHETORICAL ANALYSIS

- The speech itself is an example of **hypophoria**: Hamlet raises questions and then answers them

- "Slings and arrows of outrageous fortune" is an example of **personification**: granting human qualities to non-human entities (in this case, fortune)

ANALYSIS (CONTINUED)

- "To take arms against a sea of troubles" is an example of a **mixed metaphor**

- "That flesh is heir to" is an example of **synecdoche**: "flesh" stands in for "human beings"

- "For in that sleep what dreams may come..." is the beginning of Hamlet's description of a **double-bind**, in which there is no desirable outcome

- "Shuffled off this mortal coil" is an example of a **euphemism** for death

- "Must give us pause" is an example of Hamlet building a **rapport** (relationship) with his audience

- "For who would bear..." begins a list of life's challenges; Hamlet may be arranging his complaints in **order of importance**, as "law's delay" (a reference to the lack of justice for King Hamlet's murder) comes near to the end of the list

- This list is a kind of **invective** (tirade) against life itself

- Hamlet uses **loaded words** like "calamity," "despised," and "insolence"—words with strong emotional associations

- "Bare bodkin" is an example of **alliteration**

- "Who would fardels bear..." is an example of **commoratio**, as Hamlet begins to make the same point for the second time

- "The dread of something after death" is a reference to a shared fear—an element of the **collective unconscious**

- "Undiscovered country" is an example of a **metaphor** for the unknown of the afterlife

- "And makes us rather bear those ills we have" has given rise to the following **aphorism**, or saying: "Better the devil you know than the devil you don't"

- "Thus conscience" begins a **transitional expression** that introduces the speech's conclusion

- "And enterprises of great pitch and moment...lose the name of action" is an example of subtle **editorializing**; Hamlet is using the speech to justify his failure to act

CRAM QUIZ
Case Study: *Hamlet*'s "To Be or Not to Be" Speech

QUESTION 1

Hypophoria is a literary technique in which the speaker

(A) raises questions and then dismisses them
(B) raises objections and then overrules them
(C) raises questions and then answers them
(D) makes points and then disputes them
(E) makes plans and then cancels them

QUESTION 2

Attributing human qualities to a non-human creature or object is called

(A) synecdoche
(B) alliteration
(C) onomatopoeia
(D) personification
(E) ridiculous

QUESTION 3

A transitional expression

(A) modifies a noun
(B) links two sentences or ideas
(C) expresses numerical scope
(D) adds information about a preceding phrase
(E) is a clause that could stand alone as a complete sentence

QUESTION 4

Commoratio is a literary device in which the speaker

(A) refuses the same course of action several times
(B) asks the same question several times
(C) makes the same point several times
(D) rebuts the same argument several times
(E) issues the same insult several times

QUESTION 5

Using "hands" to mean "workers" is an example of

(A) metonymy
(B) synecdoche
(C) soliloquy
(D) aphorism
(E) metaphor

QUESTION 6

The "collective unconscious" refers to

(A) national mythology
(B) an individual's personal fears and anxieties
(C) a common goal
(D) universal fears and anxieties
(E) when a whole lot of people faint at the same time

QUESTION 7

A character offering his or her perspective on events is called

(A) meiosis
(B) establishing a rapport
(C) being a sympathetic character
(D) digressing
(E) editorializing

QUESTION 8

The relationship between the speaker or writer and the audience is called

(A) rapport
(B) foil
(C) denouement
(D) meiosis
(E) personification

ANSWERS

1. C
2. D
3. B
4. C
5. B
6. D
7. E
8. A

LITERARY ANALYSIS
More Testable Terms

LITERARY DIVERSITY

TWO TYPES OF ACTION

Some elements of narration demonstrate how characters usually behave, and other elements demonstrate how characters behave in particular circumstances.

Fixed action	• Action that shows how characters typically behave • An author might show this through flashback or modal writing • For example, "Every morning, Frank arose at dawn and ran twelve miles."
Moving action	• Action that shows how characters behave on a particular day • For example, "On that particular Tuesday, Frank woke up and decided that he would not go running."

SO SORRY

An **apology** is a defense of a certain idea, concept, or argument. (Don't confuse this literary term with what you might say if you accidentally let a manatee drive your best friend's car, and he crashed it.)

PENNY, NICKEL, PARADIGM

A **paradigm** is a set of values or assumptions that underpin a certain understanding. You can think of this as the prism through which an individual or a community views the world.

COMPARE AND CONTRAST

A **contrast** is the juxtaposition of one image or idea with another.

...AND THEY ALL LIVED HAPPILY EVER AFTER

An **epilogue** is the piece of writing at the end of a work. It often serves to explain how the characters' lives turned out.

VOCABULARY TO REMEMBER

HILARIOUS MIX-UPS AND SLAMMING DOORS

A **farce** is a comedy that relies on improbable plot turns. Prominent features include identical twins, mistaken identities, star-crossed lovers, near-misses, and the frequent slamming of doors.

An **aphorism** is a pithy saying. Here's one of Plato's:

"There is only one way to punish the mistaken ones—make them study."

Personification is the attribution of human qualities to a non-human creature or object.

The flowers danced in the wind.

The term **aesthetics** refers to issues of taste—specifically, the subjective experience elicited by a work of art.

Aesthetic distance is the effect that is produced when the experience of a work exists independently of its creator's experience in making it. This term can also apply to the objectively critical stance a reader brings to bear when evaluating a work.

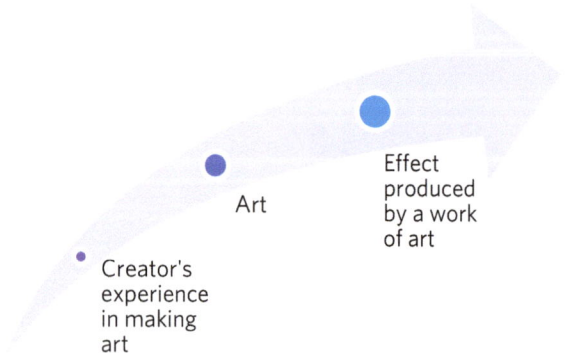

Effect produced by a work of art

Art

Creator's experience in making art

CRAM QUIZ
More Testable Terms

QUESTION 1

Aesthetics refers to

(A) issues of taste
(B) the difference between an artist's experience of creating a work and the effect that the work produces
(C) attributing human qualities to non-human creatures or objects
(D) a piece of writing at the end of a book
(E) a pithy saying

QUESTION 2

In literature, an apology is

(A) a juxtaposition between one idea or image and another
(B) attributing human qualities to non-human creatures or objects
(C) expressing regret for a mistake
(D) a pithy saying
(E) a defense of a certain idea or concept

QUESTION 3

"The mice's plot to overtake the house shall not be successful." The preceding sentence is an example of which of the following literary devices?

(A) aphorism
(B) personification
(C) epilogue
(D) apology
(E) contrast

QUESTION 4

Plot that demonstrates how characters usually behave is called

(A) paradigm
(B) epilogue
(C) moving action
(D) fixed action
(E) apology

QUESTION 5

"He who hesitates is lost" is an example of a(n)

(A) aesthetic difference
(B) aphorism
(C) epilogue
(D) personification
(E) apology

QUESTION 6

A juxtaposition between one idea or image and another is called a(n)

(A) aphorism
(B) epilogue
(C) personification
(D) contrast
(E) apology

QUESTION 7

A piece of writing at the end of a fictional work is called a(n)

(A) personification
(B) farce
(C) epilogue
(D) apology
(E) aphorism

QUESTION 8

A set of underlying values or assumptions is called a(n)

(A) paradigm
(B) epilogue
(C) moving action
(D) aphorism
(E) apology

ANSWERS

1. A
2. E
3. B
4. D
5. B
6. D
7. C
8. A

TESTING STRATEGY
Elements of the Test

KNOW THY ENEMY

EXAM STRUCTURE

The AP English Language test is divided into two parts: the multiple choice section and the essay section.

1 Multiple choice 1 hour 45% of your score	2 Essays 2 hours, 15 minutes 55% of your score

MULTIPLE CHOICE

The multiple choice section of the test is composed of 50 to 60 questions that seek to evaluate your understanding of several passages of non-fiction. The passages themselves could be about anything—science, art, politics, zombies. You don't need to have any background information on these topics. What's important is that you carefully read—and fully comprehend—the passages.

ESSAY

On the essay section, you'll write three expository essays—two analytical essays and a "synthesis" essay. (Much more on that later.)

TIMING

You'll have one hour for the multiple choice section and two hours and 15 minutes for the essay section (meaning you'll have roughly 40 minutes for each essay).

TEST-TAKING TIP

Look carefully at what the essay questions are actually asking you to do. Don't read the passage, panic, and offer 40 minutes' worth of free association about the topic. Remember that when you're asked to analyze, you're being asked to explain *how* a writer makes his or her point or communicate his or her idea.

KNOW THE SCORE

HOW THE TEST IS GRADED

As with other AP exams, the English Language test is scored on a scale of 1 to 5. Here's a translation:

- **5** • Extremely well qualified
- **4** • Well qualified
- **3** • Qualified
- **2** • Possibly qualified
- **1** • Not recommended for AP credit

SO WHAT DOES THIS MEAN FOR YOU?

As you probably already know, AP English Language is a college-level course. If you earn a high score (4 or 5) on the exam, your college might waive your freshman English requirement—leaving you more time to take electives, get a head start on the requirements for your major, or update your Facebook profile.

HOW DOES ESSAY GRADING WORK?

AP exam scorers read your essays relatively quickly, and they are asked to look at them *holistically*. This means that they're not sitting there with a calculator trying to figure out *exactly* how many comma splices are in your essay. They are drawing a *general impression* of your work—its level of clarity, sophistication, relevance, and effectiveness.

Remember that graders are aware that they are reading unrevised drafts written by high school students under tight deadlines. They're not expecting soaring prose, just competence and clarity.

TESTING STRATEGY
Tackling Multiple-Choice Questions

"THAT IS THE QUESTION"

TYPES OF QUESTIONS

Multiple choice questions will assess your understanding of a variety of short passages.

Most of the questions will relate to one of the following areas:

Language   Grammar   Rhetoric

Tone   Mood

You also may be asked questions that evaluate your understanding of footnotes.

Although there's no way to know exactly how many questions about each area you'll confront, expect to encounter more rhetoric questions than grammar questions. (But be sure to have your grammar down so that you're ready for the essays!)

WHEN *NOT* TO ANSWER A QUESTION

Generally, it's best to answer questions in order—this approach prevents you from losing track of the number of questions you've left blank (it's no fun to reach the end of your allotted time and realize that a third of your multiple choice questions are empty). At the same time, it's important to realize that you only have a minute or so to for each multiple choice question.

$$\frac{60 \text{ multiple choice questions}}{60 \text{ minutes}} = 1 \text{ question per minute}$$

That means that if a question is really tripping you up, your best bet is to skip it or guess and press on (more on guessing in a minute).

Another smart tactic is to mark questions you're unsure about as you go; if you find yourself with extra time, you can always return to them at the end of the test.

ANSWERS

I GUESS?

When you're not sure of the answer to a question, you'll probably be tempted to guess. As of 2011, you're no longer penalized for guessing—leaving an answer blank is the same as getting it wrong. So even if you have no clue, guess! If you have time, of course, eliminate as many wrong answers as you can to increase your chances.

AN ILLUSTRATIVE SCENARIO

Let's say you're working on four questions, and you're able to eliminate one answer choice from each question, but not more. If you guess on all four questions, you'll get, on average, one answer right and three wrong. You'll lose .75 points for your wrong answers and gain one point for your right answer—for a net gain of .25 points. Every little bit helps!

LEARN HOW TO READ (FOR THE AP)

You're a smart kid, and you've read a lot in your life. So you probably already know how you absorb information best—maybe you read a text through once carefully, or maybe you like to read a text twice. Maybe you skim once for a general picture and then read through more carefully a second time. Whatever your approach, it makes sense to think about it ahead of time so that you don't waste time worrying about it on Test Day.

TEST-TAKING TIP

One strategy that many students find helpful is reading through the questions—and *not* the answers—before reading the passage. You can't remember a dozen answers about a text you haven't read, but glancing at the questions ahead of time can give you a general idea of what to read for—and what to highlight—in the passage.

TESTING STRATEGY
Approaching the Essays

TYPES OF ESSAYS	MODE OF ATTACK

ESSAYS YOU'LL ENCOUNTER

You'll be asked to write three different essays on the exam. You can think of these as three different opportunities to showcase your rhetorical and analytical skills.

Essay 1

- In the first essay, you'll be asked to analyze the rhetorical tactics in a non-fiction excerpt.

Essay 2

- The second essay is a bit of a wild card—either you'll be asked to write another analytical essay **or** you'll be asked to read a short passage and support, refute, or modify its argument.

Essay 3

- The third essay is called a "synthesis" essay. For this section, you'll be asked to present your take on a given issue, integrating material that is presented alongside the question (this is the "synthesis" part). You can accept, reject, or modify the perspectives advanced in the excerpts. What is important is that you incorporate them into your own argument in a way that is relevant and insightful.

SCALING THE WALL

Essays are scored on a scale of one to nine, with one being the weakest essay score and nine being the strongest (more on these scores in a bit).

SOURCE OF THE PROBLEM

Most of the sources you'll be asked to integrate for the synthesis essay will be written passages. Occasionally, however, you'll encounter a different kind of source—such as political cartoons or graphs.

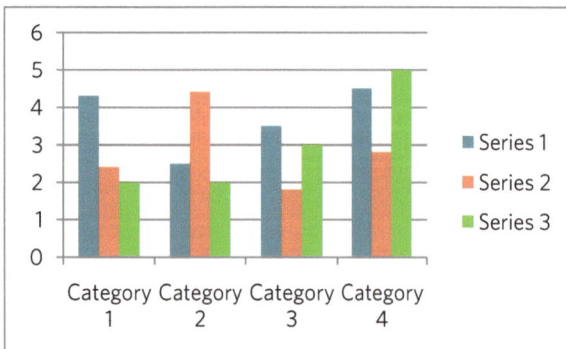

HOW ESSAYS ARE EVALUATED

Basically, your essays will be assigned a grade based on two areas—your writing and your reasoning.

- Your writing needs to be clear, mature, skillful, and grammatically correct

- Your reasoning needs to be sound: even a beautifully written essay will be marked down for shoddy logic; review the fallacies in the Rhetorical Analysis section so that you can be sure to avoid committing them

WISE WORDS

So, what does it really mean to write "maturely"? You might find yourself tempted to throw every fancy word you've ever heard into your essays, but you're better off writing clearly and competently than misusing complicated terms. General rule of thumb: write in *your* most elevated language, whatever that is.

CLARITY, CLARITY, CLARITY. IS THAT CLEAR?

The most important element of successful writing is clarity. The graders don't have to agree with your ideas—but they do have to understand them.

Try to leave yourself a few spare minutes at the end of the essay sections so that you can go over what you've written. Pretend that you're reading someone else's work. Ask yourself: would this make sense to me if I didn't already know what the writer meant?

OUTLINES: OVERRATED?

You've probably been writing essays all year in your AP English class, and you've probably approached each one with an outline. Outlines are valuable writing tools that can help you plan out a school essay in detail. But on the AP exam, consider drafting only very basic outlines for your essays—perhaps a few key ideas for each paragraph. Anything more extensive will occupy too much of your (limited!) time.

TEST-TAKING TIP

The third essay asks you to integrate given sources into an argument of your own. You can do this however you want—you can support, partially support, or totally reject the arguments—but you must cite your sources. The AP graders are flexible about how you do this, but parenthetical citation will probably save you the most time.

TESTING STRATEGY
General Tips, Tricks, and Information

GETTING READY FOR THE BIG DAY

COUNTDOWN TO THE TEST

- 3 weeks before Test Day: set a timer and write an essay in 40 minutes. The next day, go over it and try to evaluate impartially how it stacks up against essays you've written more leisurely. Try to identify problem areas: in the heat of the moment, do you make grammar mistakes? Logical fallacies? Syntactical errors? These are the areas on which to focus extra attention on Test Day.

- 2 weeks before Test Day: enhance your visual literacy by checking out some political cartoons or informational graphs. Most of the sources you'll encounter will be literary, but a few may be visual. And by now, you're probably ready for a mental break.

- 1 week before Test Day: you probably have a spelling or grammar nemesis, and now is the time to conquer it. Do you have trouble remembering how to spell "receive"? Does the word "whom" slip out at inappropriate moments? Do you have difficulty getting through a sentence without using m-dashes? (I do.) Think about what mistake you're likely to make when rushing, and then think about how you'll avoid it. One mistake isn't going to make or break you on Test Day. But the overall efficacy of your writing matters, and there's no reason to lose points on foreseeable blunders.

- The night before Test Day: Get some sleep. Really. Studies have shown that students who are adequately rested perform better than students who are not. If it is currently fewer than eight hours from the time your alarm goes off, put this guide down immediately and *go to sleep*.

FINAL TIPS AND INFORMATION

ESSAY SCORING
So what do those scores mean, anyways?

- **9** • Exceptionally well-written, insightful, and thorough. Errors, if present, are very minor.

- **8** • Extremely well-written and demonstrates an impressive command of English.

- **7** • Competent and reasonably well-developed with no egregious errors.

- **6** • Similar to a 7, though the prose may be less sophisticated and the flaws in diction and syntax more serious.

- **5** • Adequate but may be under-developed. Writing may be well-organized but ineffective.

- **4** • Responds inadequately to the question—by missing the point of the question or by making a weak or incomplete argument.

- **3** • Does not adequately answer the question and may be poorly organized and poorly written.

- **2** • Does not analyze the passage or synthesize the sources. It may summarize them instead.

- **1** • Profoundly limited and may be nearly incomprehensible.

AND REMEMBER...

The English Language exam is not like other AP exams. Although a lot of material comes up year after year (high school students of the next millennium will still be asked to evaluate an author's tone, and a solid command of grammar and mechanics will always be crucial), the bottom line is that there is no way to know *exactly* what you'll be asked on the English Language test. This isn't biology or calculus—there's not a finite amount of material, and the essays don't have a right answer.

So the bad news is this: memorization is only going to get you so far. At the end of the day, the ability to read and write skillfully is the most important element of AP English Language success.

The good news is that there's no single approach to doing well. Different students can tackle the same material from wildly divergent perspectives; as long as these students all write persuasively and artfully, they'll all do well. There are as many ways to write brilliant essays as there are brilliant students to write them.

CRUNCH KIT
AP English Language in Four Pages (Page 1)

PARTS OF SPEECH

- A **noun** names a person, place, thing, or idea
- A **pronoun** replaces a noun
- An **adjective** modifies a noun
- A **verb** is a word that expresses being or action
- An **adverb** modifies a verb
- An **interjection** is a part of speech that doesn't fit into the other conventional parts of speech
- A **conjunction** links one phrase to another
- A **preposition** is a short word that indicates position, direction, or location
- An **article** is a word that functions with a noun to indicate the reference a noun is making
- An **indefinite article** refers to any member of a group, and a **definite article** refers to a particular member of a group

VERBS

- A **linking verb** indicates what something is, was, or will be
- An **action verb** indicates what something is, was, or will be doing
- An **auxiliary verb** is a verb that serves a linking function in a sentence
- A **participle** is a verb form that can be used as an adjective
- A **present participle** is a participle in the present tense
- A **past participle** is a participle in the past tense
- A **transitive verb** is a verb that takes a direct object
- An **intransitive verb** is a verb that takes no direct object
- A **gerund** is a verb form ending with the letters "-ing"
- A verb's **tense** expresses whether the action happened in the past, present, or future
- A verb's **aspect** expresses the action's relationship to the passage of time, particularly whether the action is completed, continuing, or repeated
- The **infinitive** is a verb's uninflected form
- A **split infinitive** occurs when another word comes between the word "to" and the uninflected form of the verb
- An **irregular verb** is a verb whose conjugation deviates from normal rules

NOUNS

- A **concrete noun** names a thing that can be perceived by the senses
- An **abstract noun** names a quality, characteristic, or idea
- A **common noun** does not name a particular person, place, or thing
- A **proper noun** names a particular person, place, or thing
- A **collective noun** names a group
- An **adjectival noun** is a noun that functions as an adjective

ADJECTIVES

- A **limiting adjective** indicates whose, what, or how many
- A **quantifier** is an adjective that expresses numerical scope
- An **adjective phrase** is a phrase that modifies a noun
- An **adjective clause** contains a subject and a verb, begins with a relative adjective or relative adverb, and functions as an adjective
- An **interrogative adjective** is an interrogative pronoun that is used as an adjective

ADVERBS

- An **adverb clause** is a clause that modifies a verb

CONJUNCTIONS

- A **coordinating conjunction** joins two items of equal syntactical importance
- **Correlative conjunctions** are pairs of conjunctions that work together to correlate two items
- A **subordinating conjunction** introduces a dependent clause

PUNCTUATION

- A **colon** (:) is a punctuation mark that indicates a pause and that other information will follow
- A **semicolon** (;) is a punctuation mark that serves to separate items in a list containing internal punctuation or to separate two independent clauses
- A **comma** (,) is a punctuation mark used to separate clauses, enclose parenthetical expressions, or separate coordinate adjectives
- **Ellipses** (...) indicate that words are missing, as from a quote
- An **Oxford comma** precedes the conjunction ("and") in a list

CRUNCH KIT
AP English Language in Four Pages (Page 2)

STYLE

- **Syntax** is the way in which words are arranged to form phrases, clauses, and sentences
- **Apposition** is putting two phrases together in order to give additional information
- **Modal writing** tells what usually happened
- **Parallelism** is expressing similarly two or more items of equal syntactical importance

SENTENCE ELEMENTS

- A **sentence fragment** is a string of words that does not contain both a subject and a verb
- A **sentence** contains a subject and a verb and expresses a complete thought
- A **declarative sentence** is a sentence that makes a statement
- A **negative sentence** is a sentence that denies that a statement is true
- An **interrogative sentence** is a sentence that asks a question
- An **exclamatory sentence** emphatically expresses emotion
- An **imperative sentence** expresses a command
- A **sentence** has a compound subject when two or more subjects share a verb
- A **complement** is a word, phrase, or clause that is necessary to complete a sentence's meaning
- A **complex sentence** contains an independent clause joined by one or more independent clause(s)
- A **compound sentence** is composed of two independent clauses
- A **simple sentence** is an independent clause
- A **predicate** is the part of the sentence that modifies the subject
- A **predicate nominative** indicates what the subject is
- A **predicate adjective** follows a linking verb and indicates something about the subject
- A **parenthetical expression** gives non-essential information
- A **subordinate** (or **dependent**) **clause** is a clause that could not stand on its own as a sentence
- An **independent clause** is a clause that could stand on its own as a complete sentence
- To **modify** is to give additional information about a word
- An **object** is the sentence element that is involved in the performance of the verb
- A **direct object** is the thing or person acted upon by a transitive verb
- An **indirect object** serves as the recipient of the direct object

WORDS

- An **antonym** is a word with an opposite definition of that of another word
- A **synonym** is word with a similar definition to that of another word
- A word's **denotation** is its literal definition
- A word's **connotation** is the set of feelings and associations it evokes
- A **comparative** establishes a relationship between two nouns
- A **superlative** expresses the idea that a noun possesses a certain quality to the highest degree possible
- An **antecedent** is the term to which a pronoun refers
- A **zeugma** is a word that links two words or phrases
- **Morphology** is the form words take
- **Interpolation** is the addition of words to a quotation for clarity
- **Mechanics** are the technical details of writing
- A **paragraph** is a sentence or set of sentences that expresses one well-developed idea
- A **contraction** is a word that is shortened by the elimination of letters
- An **affix** is a word element added to a root word
- A **prefix** is an affix that precedes a root word
- A **suffix** is an affix that follows a root word
- **Polarity** is the indication of affirmation or negation
- An **aphorism** is a pithy saying

ELEMENTS OF ENGLISH

- **Standard English** is grammatically correct English
- **Non-standard English** is a diverse set of conventions that are discernibly different from standard English
- **Informal English** is the English speakers use in their daily lives
- A **neologism** is a new word
- A **shibboleth** is a word that reveals or hints at the speaker's geographic origin
- **Slang** is a kind of language made up of short-term coinages and figures of speech
- **Etymology** is the study of word origins
- **Idiolect** is the language pattern unique to an individual
- **Dialect** is the language pattern shared by a region
- **Latinate diction** is the use of words of Latin origin
- A **semantic change** is a change in a word's meaning
- **Germanic diction** is the use of words of German origin

CRUNCH KIT
AP English Language in Four Pages (Page 3)

QUESTIONS

- An **embedded question** is a part of a sentence that would be a query if it were on its own
- A **rhetorical** (or **hypothetical**) **question** is a question that does not seek an answer
- A **leading question** is a question that suggests its own answer
- **Erotema** is a question asked in order to make an argument

GRAMMAR PROBLEMS

- A **dangling modifier** occurs when it is ambiguous which part of the sentence a clause is modifying
- A **run-on sentence** is an ungrammatical sentence in which two sentences are combined without proper punctuation
- **Hypercorrection** is when a concern for grammatical correctness contributes to grammatical problems

MOODS

- **Moods** are verb forms that express whether an action might have happened, actually happened, or should have happened
- The **declarative mood** is the normal form of a verb
- The **imperative** is the form verbs take when instructions are given
- The **subjunctive** expresses a desire, command, or wish
- The **conditional** expresses that an action might happen or might have happened

RHETORICAL TERMS

- A **cliché** is a saying that has been used so often it has lost its appeal
- **Hyperbole** is the rhetorical strategy of using exaggeration
- **Invective** is the denouncement of a person, place, thing, or idea
- A **paradox** is a self-contradicting assertion
- A **rebuttal** is a response to an argument
- An **epithet** is a descriptive phrase that stands in place of a name
- An **analogy** is a comparison of one situation to another
- A **causal argument** advances a position about why a phenomenon occurs
- An **argument of evaluation** advances a position about the merits of a particular policy
- An **argument of definition** advances a position about the way we understand, categorize, or discuss a certain thing
- A **proposal argument** advances a solution for a problem
- **Auxesis** is a gradual heightening of words' intensity
- **Bdelygmia** is a litany of insults
- **Tapinosis** is undignified language that demeans a person or thing
- **Synathroesmus** is a listing of adjectives

QUOTATIONS

- A **broken quotation** is a quotation that is interrupted, usually by a dialogue tag
- **Sic** is a word that is used to indicate that irregularities in quotations were found in the original text
- **Indirect discourse** is the reporting of what someone said in another context without the use of quotation marks
- **Direct discourse** is the reporting of what someone said in another context by using quotation marks

RHETORICAL APPEALS

- **Ethos** is an appeal to authority
- **Pathos** is an appeal to emotion
- **Logos** is an appeal to logic
- **Bathos** is an attempt at pathos that goes too far and becomes absurd
- **Bandwagon appeal** relies on the notion that something should be done or believed because many people do or believe it
- **Snob appeal** relies on the notion that something should be done or believed because elites do or believe it
- **Plain-folks appeal** relies on the notion that something should be done or believed because ordinary people do or believe it
- **Begging the question** is assuming one's conclusion in the course of an argument
- **Dogmatism** is arrogance in asserting an opinion
- **Testimonial appeal** is using a well-known person to advertise a product or endorse an argument
- **Circular reasoning** is giving no particular reasons to support one's argument
- A **concession** is an admission of a disputed point
- **Absolute certainty** is ironclad sureness
- **Ignoring the issue** is directing the conversation away from the intended topic
- **Righteous indignation** is moralistic anger

LOGIC

- **Associational logic** is the intuitive process of reasoning
- **Formal logic** is the rational process of reasoning (also called **ratiocination**)
- **Deductive structure** is the form of reasoning in which a conclusion is articulated and then shown to adhere to a particular premise
- **Inductive structure** is the form of reasoning in which an observation is made and then a conclusion is drawn from it
- A **syllogism** is a form of logical argument in which a conclusion is inferred from two premises
- A **tautology** occurs when something is stated twice unnecessarily
- A **double-bind** is a situation in which there is no desirable outcome

CRUNCH KIT
AP English Language in Four Pages (Page 4)

WRITING TERMS

- **Explication** is the process of making the implicit explicit
- **Jargon** is inaccessible, overly technical language
- **Personal myth** is the self-concept that a narrator or author presents
- **Propaganda** is a didactic piece of work that seeks to persuade a reader to take a particular stance
- **Unity** is the overall coherence of a work
- An **anecdote** is a brief story, often illustrative
- A **thesis** is the argument of a piece of writing
- **Context** is the background in which a fact or event is situated
- An **implication** is something that a writer suggests but does not state directly
- A **euphemism** is a way of phrasing something so as to soften its impact
- **Exposition** is a piece of writing that offers an introduction to and description of a topic
- A **transitional expression** is a phrase used to connect ideas
- A **proposition** is a statement phrased in debatable form
- A **totalizing statement** is a sweeping statement that deals in absolutes
- A **contrast** is a juxtaposition of one image with another
- **Interpretation** is the general explanation of a text's meaning

FALLACIES

- A **fallacy** is an argument that provides shoddy or false reasoning in defense of its conclusion
- **Faulty causality** (also called the conflation of correlation and causation) is the assumption that because one event followed another, the first caused the second
- The *ad hominem* **fallacy** is an attempt to discredit an opponent's view by attacking his or her character
- The **either-or fallacy** is thinking of a problem as having only two possible solutions
- **Misrepresentation of references** is taking an opponent's argument out of context

VOICE

- **Passive voice** uses the verb "to be," generally in conjunction with the past tense of a verb ("was made")
- **Active voice** avoids use of the verb "to be" ("made")
- **Point of view** is the perspective from which a narrative is conveyed to a reader
- **Overwriting** is the use of language that is unnecessarily wordy or elaborate
- **Understatement** is the rhetorical strategy of restraint
- **Tone** is an author's attitude toward his or her subject matter

ELEMENTS OF PLOT

- A **catalytic event** is a precipitating event that leads to a climax
- **Catharsis** is an emotional climax or breakdown
- **Rising action** is the part of the plot that precedes the climax
- **Falling action** is the part of the plot that follows the climax
- A **frame story** contains other, usually shorter, narratives within it
- A **subplot** is a narrative that exists within a broader narrative arc

ELEMENTS OF CHARACTER

- A **protagonist** is the main character
- An **antagonist** is a figure that challenges the protagonist
- A **flat character** is a one-dimensional character
- A **round character** is a multi-dimensional character
- A **stock character** is a character that is frequently found in literature

LITERARY TERMS

- **Gestalt** is the entirety of the effect of a work of literature
- **Verbal irony** occurs when a speaker or writer states the opposite of what is meant
- **Dramatic irony** occurs when the readers or audience knows something a character does not
- **Situational irony** occurs when circumstances unfold in an unexpected way
- **Aesthetic distance** is the effect that is produced by a piece of art that exists independently of the creator's experience in making it
- **Negative capability** is receptivity to ambiguity and mystery
- The **objective correlative** is the idea that a well-selected image or chain of events can serve as a formula for a particular emotion
- An **apology** is the defense of a certain idea, argument, or concept
- **In media res** is the literary strategy of starting a story in the middle of the action
- A **paradigm** is an example or a set of assumptions that underpin a certain understanding
- A **convention** is a familiar rule or feature of literature
- A **stock situation** is a situation that is commonly found in literature
- A **symbol** is an image that contains a meaning beyond its literal function
- **Synecdoche** is using a part to refer to a whole
- A **tragedy** is a narrative structure in which a character suffers an irredeemable downfall

DemiDec

CRUNCH KIT
List of Lists

10 TOUGH TERMS TO REMEMBER

Aesthetic distance	The effect created when an artistic work exists independently of the author's experience in creating it
Affix	Something added to a root word
Apostrophe	The use of direct address to an absent person or entity
Apposition	Putting two sentences together in order to give additional information
Deus ex machina	A last-minute rescue or resolution
In media res	The literary strategy of beginning a story in the middle of the action
Meiosis	Understatement
Propaganda	A didactic piece of writing that seeks to persuade
Syllogism	A form of logical reasoning in which a conclusion is inferred from two or more premises
Synecdoche	Taking a part for a whole

8 WRITING MISTAKES TO AVOID

Cause-and-effect fallacy	The conflation of correlation and causation
Cliché	A phrase or image that has become hackneyed from overuse
Hypercorrection	Don't make grammatical mistakes in a misguided effort to be grammatically correct! Your top priority is clarity
Ignoring context	Context is the background against which a fact or event is situated. Remember to consider the context of any passage you're analyzing—and to put your own evidence into context when writing your own arguments
Ignoring parallelism	Remember to express sentence elements of similar syntactical importance similarly
Incorrect use of whom	An easy trick: think about whether "him/her" or "he/she" would be appropriate in place of "whom";if it's "him/her," go with whom and if it's "he/she," stick with who
Overwriting	Don't use overly elaborate or wordy language
Redundancy	Avoid repetitiveness

9 HIGH PRIORITY TERMS

Allegory	A work in which the characters, objects, and settings are meant to correspond to a second set of objects, characters, and settings outside the work itself
Antagonist	A character who thwarts the protagonist
Catalytic event	In a literary work, the precipitating action that leads to the climax
Climax	The point of highest tension in a literary work
Convention	A familiar rule or feature of literature
Interpretation	The general explanation of a text's meaning
Irony	Know the three kinds: dramatic (readers/audience knowing something a character does not), verbal (a writer or speaker stating the opposite of what is meant), and situational (circumstances unfolding in an unexpected way)
Symbol	An image that contains a meaning beyond the literal
Theme	A recurring pattern, idea, or preoccupation in a work

4 GRAMMAR PITFALLS

Ambiguous reference of pronouns	A pronoun that refers confusingly to two or more antecedents
Dangling modifier	When it is ambiguous what part of the sentence a word, phrase, or clause is modifying
Sentence fragment	A string of words that does not contain both a subject and a verb
Squinting modifier	A modifier that is positioned in such a way that it may be taken to modify two verbs

CRUNCH KIT
List of Lists

9 MEDIUM PRIORITY TERMS

Digression	A passage that is not tightly tied to the overarching theme or narration
Gestalt	The entirety of the effect of a work of literature
Negative capability	Receptivity to ambiguity and mystery
Objective correlative	The notion that a well-selected image or chain of events can serve as a formula for a particular emotion
Paradigm	An example, or a set of assumptions underpinning an understanding
Point of view	The perspective from which a narrative is communicated to an audience
Refutation	The anticipation and rebuttal of an opposing argument
Satire	A work that criticizes the failings of a person, society, or institution by way of ridicule
Tone	An author's attitude toward his or her subject matter

8 TERMS NOT TO CONFUSE

Connotation	The feelings and associations that a word evokes
Denotation	The definition of a word
Deductive reasoning	The form of reasoning in which a conclusion is articulated and then shown to adhere to a particular premise
Inductive reasoning	The form of reasoning in which an observation is made and then a conclusion is drawn from it
Germanic diction	Words originating from German (usually blunter and shorter than their Latin counterparts)
Latinate diction	Words originating from Latin (usually technical, scientific, and medical)
Objective	Examining facts without bringing to bear personal experience
Subjective	Examining facts by bringing to bear personal experience

10 MEDIUM PRIORITY TERMS

Concession	The admission of a disputed point
Dialect	The speech patterns unique to a particular region
Dogmatism	Arrogance in asserting an opinion
Exposition	A piece of writing that offers explanation
Glittering generalities	Words that elicit strongly positive emotional connotations
Idiolect	The speech patterns unique to a particular individual
Loaded words	Words with strong emotional associations
Rapport	The relationship a writer builds with his or her audience
Rebuttal	A response to an argument
Transitional expressions	Phrases that writers use to connect ideas

8 RHETORICAL PROBLEMS AND POSSIBILITIES

Ad hominem fallacy	Attacking an argument by attacking the character of the person advancing the argument
Artistic appeal	A statement that makes a rational appeal
Begging the question	Assuming one's conclusion in the course of one's argument
Circular reasoning	Giving no particular reasons to support one's claim, other than variations of the claim itself
Dogmatism	Arrogance in asserting an opinion
Either-or fallacy	Thinking of a problem as having only two possible solutions
Fallacy	Providing shoddy or false reasoning in defense of a conclusion
Inartistic appeal	A statement that appeals to hard evidence

CRUNCH KIT
List of Lists

10 LOWER PRIORITY TERMS

Aphorism	A pithy saying
Apology	A defense of a certain idea or argument
Auxesis	A gradual heightening of the intensity of words' meaning
Bdelygmia	A litany of insults
Commoratio	Repeating the same point several times using different words
Hypophoria	Raising questions and then answering them
Implication	Something a writer suggests but does not state directly
Semantics	The study of meaning
Tapinosis	Undignified language that demeans a person or thing
Tautology	In logic, something that is stated twice unnecessarily

10 IMPORTANT RHETORICAL APPEALS

Associational logic	The intuitive process of reasoning
Bandwagon appeal	Implying or stating that many people endorse a particular product or position
Bathos	An appeal to emotion that goes too far and becomes absurd
Ethos	An appeal to authority
Formal logic	The rational process of reasoning (also called ratiocination)
Hyperbole	The rhetorical strategy of exaggeration
Logos	An appeal to logic
Pathos	An appeal to emotion
Plain-folks appeal	Implying or stating that the "common man" endorses a particular product or position
Snob appeal	Implying or stating that the sophisticated and elite endorse a particular product or position
Testimonial appeal	Implying or stating that an important person or group endorses a particular product or position

11 LOWER PRIORITY TERMS

Collective unconscious	The idea that there is a universal awareness that gives us shared fears and desires
Contraction	A word that is shortened by the elimination of letters
Conventional symbol	A symbol that is specific to a particular nation or region
Idiom	A common figure of speech that is not easily translatable into another language
Inflection	The process by which words change form
Interpolation	Words added to a quote for clarity
Invective	The denouncement of a person, place, thing or idea
Meta-fiction	A narrative that exists outside of—or on top of—another
Soliloquy	In drama, a speech—usually delivered when a character is alone onstage
Totalizing statement	A statement that deals in absolutes
Universal symbol	A symbol that cuts across nations and cultures

5 CRUCIAL GRAMMAR PAIRS

Action verb	A verb which establishes that something was done, is done, or will be done
Linking verb	A verb which establishes a relationship between the subject and a term in the predicate (does not show action)
Antonym	A word with the opposite meaning of that of another word
Synonym	A word with a similar meaning to that of another word
Coordinating conjunction	A conjunction that joins two items of equal syntactical importance
Correlative conjunction	Pairs of conjunctions that work together to correlate two items
Dependent clause	A clause that could not stand on its own as a complete sentence
Independent clause	A clause that could stand on its own as a complete sentence
Intransitive verb	A verb that describes what something or someone was, is, or will be doing
Transitive verb	A verb that describes what something or someone was, is, or will be

CRUNCH KIT
List of Lists

15 LITERARY TERMS

Denouement	Another term for "falling action"
Falling action	The part of the plot that follows the climax
Farce	A comedy that relies on improbable or extravagant plot twists
Fixed action	Action that shows us how characters usually behave
Lampoon	To skewer or satirize
Motif	A recurring idea, image, or dynamic
Moving action	Action that shows us how characters behave under a certain set of circumstances
Parody	A spoof
Pastiche	A parody on a small scale
Plot	The events in a work of literature
Rising action	The part of the plot that precedes the climax
Theme	A recurring idea or preoccupation within a text
Tragedy	A narrative structure in which a character suffers an irreversible downfall
Tragic flaw	A quality that leads inevitably to a character's downfall
Travesty	In literature, the handling of a solemn subject in a crass or mocking way

9 TIPS TO REMEMBER FOR YOUR ESSAYS

Avoid "stringy style"	"Stringy style" results from an overreliance on words like "and" and "so"; make sure your sentences are grammatical and concise
Colloquialism	A commonly used figure of speech; these are considered inappropriate for formal writing
Diction	The selection and arrangement of your words
Digression	A passage that is not tightly tied to the overarching argument; the AP essays are short and your time is limited, so it's best to avoid these
Economy	Using only the necessary number of words
Phrasing	Be attentive to the way your sentences are working together
Thesis	The argument that your essay is making; you'll want to articulate it within the first paragraph of your piece
Unity	Coherence
Word choice	An author's selection of words; pay attention to yours

6 DIFFERENT ANALYTICAL APPROACHES

Deconstructionist literary criticism	Seeks to uncover the contradictions inherent within the text
Feminist literary criticism	Examines the work from a feminist perspective
Formalist literary criticism	Examines the inherent features of the text, such as style, plot, and character
Freudian literary criticism	Examines the text from a Freudian perspective
Marxist literary criticism	Examines the work from a class perspective
Moral literary criticism	Examines the ethical implications of the text

9 KINDS OF CHARACTERS

Antagonist	A character who challenges, thwarts, or frustrates the protagonist
Antihero	A character lacking the qualities necessary for heroism
Fixed character	A character who does not exhibit a capacity for change
Flat character	A one-dimensional character
Foil	Serves to highlight a particular quality of another character
Moving character	A character who exhibits the capacity for change
Protagonist	Main character
Round character	A multidimensional character
Stock character	A character who is commonly found in literature

CRUNCH KIT
List of Lists

8 WAYS TO TELL A STORY

Epiphany	A sudden realization or reversal
First-person narrator	A narrator who is a character
First-person observer	A narrator who is a minor character in a story
First-person participant	A narrator who is a major character in a story
Flashback	In fiction, the technique of showing events that happened prior to the present action of the story
Foreshadowing	When the text suggests an event will happen later in the plot
Projection	When a narrator's emotional state informs descriptions of the setting
Unreliable narrator	A narrator who does not serve as an accurate witness to his or her own story

6 KINDS OF LITERATURE

African American literature	The body of work produced by African American literature; important contributors include Alice Walker and Walter Mosley
Central American literature	The body of work produced by Central American authors; important contributors include Miguel Angel Asturias and Octavio Paz
Hispanic American literature	The body of work produced by Hispanic American authors; important contributors include Junot Diaz and Sandra Cisneros
Native American literature	The body of work produced by Native American authors; important contributors include Louise Erdrich and Sherman Alexie
South American literature	The body of work produced by South American authors; important contributors include Gabriel Garcia Marquez and Roberto Bolano
Young adult literature	Literature written for or marketed to adolescents

5 TRICKY PUNCTUATION MARKS

Colon (:)	A punctuation mark used to indicate a pause; followed by enumeration, elaboration, or explanation
Comma (,)	A punctuation mark used to separate clauses, enclose parenthetical words or phrases, and separate coordinate adjectives
Ellipses (…)	Punctuation that indicates that words are missing, as from a quote
Oxford comma	Immediately precedes the conjunction ("and") in a list
Semicolon (;)	A punctuation mark used to separate independent clauses or internally punctuated items in a list

5 TYPES OF LANGUAGE

Abstract language	Language that refers to the intangible
Concrete language	Language that refers to the tangible
Elevated language	Formal, elaborate language
Figurative language	Language that refers beyond the literal
Literal language	Language that means exactly what it says
Vernacular	Language that is particular to a region or culture

FINAL TIPS AND ABOUT THE AUTHOR

FINAL TIPS

- Remember to identify your grammar trouble spots ahead of time
- Get enough sleep before Test Day; ideally, get enough sleep the whole *week* before Test Day
- For your test essays, make only bare-bones outlines
- Remember that you will see more questions about rhetoric than about grammar...
- And remember that your grammar competence will be evaluated in your essays
- Don't worry too much; you are young, it's almost summer, and this is—as they say—only a test
- English is a great subject—have some fun with it!

ABOUT THE AUTHOR

Jennifer duBois holds a B.A. in political science and philosophy from Tufts University and an M.F.A. in English from the Iowa Writers' Workshop. She is also a 2009-2011 Stegner Fellow at Stanford University. Her stories have appeared in *The Northwest Review, The South Carolina Review,* and *The Florida Review,* and she is currently at work on a forbidding book about the former Soviet Union. When she's not writing, she enjoys political blogs, sandwiches, and other people's forbidding books about the former Soviet Union.

ABOUT THE EDITOR

DEAN SCHAFFER

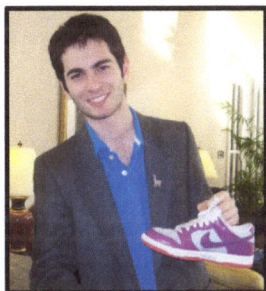

Since leading Los Angeles's Taft High School to a national Academic Decathlon championship and shipping off to Stanford University, Dean Schaffer has designed and developed DemiDec's signature Power Guides and Cram Kits. Over the years, he has maintained his affinity for a variety of metaphorical hats (editing, writing, and layout, especially), non-metaphorical sunglasses (Aviators, always), and the guitar (Fender, usually). When he's not editing, Dean is generally looking for something nearby to edit—dont we all luv to find speling erors?

In his spare time, Dean ponders whether he'll ever be able to handle the luxury of spare time; luckily, he avoids this metaphysical quandary altogether by choosing not to affiliate himself with relaxation of any form. Instead, he occupies himself with songwriting, playing guitar, and parallel structure-ing. When he isn't doing those things, he's considering the merits of democratic elections, oligarchic disinterestedness, and delicious gouda cheese.

ABOUT DEMIDEC

THE DEMIDEC STORY

Since 1994, DemiDec has been the worldwide leader in student-centered learning experiences, from its curriculum for the Academic Decathlon in the United States to its college prep academies in Asia. DemiDec now brings its unique approach—and its mascot, the alpaca—to a whole new realm: AP and SAT materials.

To learn more, visit www.demidec.com.

ABOUT THE WORLD SCHOLAR'S CUP

Six subjects. Four events. Teams of three.

DemiDec's World Scholar's Cup is an international team academic tournament with thousands of participants in 30 countries. It centers on a different them each year—from the Frontier to the Fall of Empires. Events include team debate, a scholar's bowl, and more.

Discover this year's theme, learn more about the program, and sign up for free at www.scholarscup.org.

SPREAD THE CRAM!

Visit www.demidec.com to find out how you can become part of the DemiDec Street Team and raise money for yourself or your school.